The Gospel according to Hollywood

The Gospel according to Hollywood

Greg Garrett

Westminster John Knox Press
LOUISVILLE • LONDON

© 2007 Greg Garrett

Scripture quotations, unless otherwise indicated, are from the New Revised Standard Version of the Bible, copyright © 1989 by the Division of Christian Education of the National Council of the Churches of Christ in the U.S.A., and used by permission.

Book design by Sharon Adams
Cover design by designpointinc.com

First edition
Published by Westminster John Knox Press
Louisville, Kentucky

This book is printed on acid-free paper that meets the American National Standards Institute Z39.48 standard. ∞

PRINTED IN THE UNITED STATES OF AMERICA

07 08 09 10 11 12 13 14 15 16 — 10 9 8 7 6 5 4 3 2 1

Library of Congress Cataloging-in-Publication Data

Garrett, Greg.
    The Gospel according to Hollywood / Greg Garrett — 1st ed.
      p. cm.
    ISBN-13: 978-0-664-23052-4 (alk. paper)
    ISBN-10: 0-664-23052-0 (alk. paper)
    1. Motion pictures—Religious aspects—Christianity. I. Title.

    PN1995.5.G37 2007
    261.5'7—dc22

                             2006051886

*To the students, faculty, staff, and alumni of the
Episcopal Seminary of the Southwest, Austin, Texas*

Contents

Preface   ix

Introduction   xiii

1. Faith and Belief: Does God Exist?   1
2. The Trinity: If God Exists, What Kind of God *Is* God?   24
3. Sin and Death: If God Is Good, Where Did Evil Come From?   48
4. Grace and Redemption: If the World Is Filled with Evil,
   How Do We Find Salvation?   82
5. Peace and Justice: How Do We Live a Righteous Life?   108
6. The Church and the Christian: What Does It Mean to Be a
   Believer in Contemporary America?   144

Notes   166

Preface

*R*owan Williams has said that theology is what we do when we try to talk about God, and it is never final. I think truer words were never spoken. With each theological book I write, I find my thinking refined by those minds and souls with whom I've come into contact, living and dead, and what I can say about this book is that *The Gospel according to Hollywood* is a snapshot of my current understanding of God and my attempt to synthesize what I know and feel in hopes that it will be of use to others. I'm lately very much drawn to Paul Tillich's idea of dialectical theology, and my reading ranges widely and wildly; it's my hope that all of these birds will roost happily together as night falls.

Chris Seay started me down this road, and continues to walk alongside me. His insights and encouragement have been instrumental in my writing this book. Thanks, Buddy.

At Westminster John Knox, it has been a joy to work with David Dobson, who talked me through several ideas to reach the concept for the book I really wanted to write for him. I also want to thank David Maxwell, my editor at The Thoughtful Christian, the Westminster John Knox Web site, for which I have lately had a chance to think through my reactions to some of these films and theological issues. Thanks also to Ralph Wood and Mark Pinsky, authors who preceded me in this series with fine books and who answered my questions about it with patience and encouragement.

My greatest debt this time is to my faculty and friends at the Episcopal Theological Seminary of the Southwest, where in the fall of 2004, in midlife, I made the radical and completely blessed step of beginning study for the Master of Divinity degree. Anthony Baker has been my guide to the church fathers and Radical Orthodoxy, my first formal theological trainer, and I could not have been luckier in that fact. Chapters 1 and 2 were developed for a class Tony and I did together on theology and film, and they are much improved for his attention to them. Cynthia Briggs-Kittredge and Ray Pickett are fine scholars who taught me new tools to bring to the study of the Bible and confirmed in me the need to read through the lenses of justice and inclusion. I'm grateful to Corinne Ware and Mary Earle, writers whom I have both read and met in the classroom, for expanding my understanding of Christian spiritual practice, Susan Dolan-Henderson for introducing me to Stanley Hauerwas (his work, not Stanley himself), Steve Bishop for reminding me how to read a story, Alan Gregory for my formal introduction to church history, and Charlie Cook and Roger Paynter for urging me to look for the gospel in everything; "Where is the gospel in this?" is the most important question I know. Finally, my advisor Russell Schulz has walked with me through challenging times with grace and humor, and encouraged me to do the work God has given me. Thanks to all of you for the good work you do, and for the way your work has shaped my life for the better. This book as well is immeasurably better because of you.

I'm also beholden to the other members of my seminary community, who have been a *koinōnia* and an *ekklēsia* for me—perhaps the most important of my life so far. At one time or another Don Smith, Joe Behen, Ken Malcolm, Lisa Miller, De Freeman, Carissa Baldwin, Kevin Schubert, Heath Abel, Cathy Boyd, Chad Vaughn, Hunt Priest, Roger Joslin, Liz Muñoz, and Bob Kinney and I have had memorable conversations about movies, faith, and life. Many others have said things in class or in conversation that have shaped me. Again, I'm grateful.

Thanks to all those friends and family who've talked movies, theology, or both with me, especially Greg Rickel, Tom Hanks, Scott Walker, Philip and Ali Newell, my sons Jake and Chandler, and Tinamarie Garrett. The classes I teach at Baylor University have given me the opportunity to discuss movies like *Magnolia*, *Crash*, *Unforgiven*, and *Do the Right Thing*, and I'm indebted to my students for their insights, affection, and support. At Baylor, I also owe thanks to the administrators, particularly Provost Randall O'Brien and English Department Chair Maurice Hunt, who affirmed my call to attend seminary and who made it possible to simultaneously continue my service as a Baylor faculty member. Much of this book had beginnings in a research leave granted me by the university in the spring of 2005.

Thanks to my supportive communities of faith: my beloved St. James Episcopal Church and the Rev. Dr. Greg Rickel in Austin, Texas, and Calvary Episcopal Church and the Rev. Matt Zimmerman in Bastrop, Texas, where I have served joyfully during my seminary years.

Thanks to all those folks who have heard me present my ideas about story, film, theology, and faith in lectures, workshops, classes, retreats, and other programs over the past few years. The discussions you participated in and your feedback helped to clarify much for me. Thanks to the Rev. Tim Ditchfield and the Rev. Dr. Richard Burridge for their invitation to lecture from the book in progress at the wondrous Chapel at King's College, London, and to the Rev. Canon Martyn Percy for the same opportunity at Ripon College Cuddesdon, Oxford, a sister Anglican seminary. Thanks to the parishioners of St. Paul's Episcopal Church, Waco, Texas; First Baptist Church, Austin, Texas; Saint James' Episcopal, Austin, Texas; Saint David's Episcopal, Austin, Texas; and Calvary Episcopal, Bastrop, Texas. Thanks to participants in classes and workshops at the Ghost Ranch conference centers in Santa Fe and Abiquiu, New Mexico; to the Seton Cove Spirituality Center, Austin, Texas; to premed and med-school students, high school campers, and Episcopal Diocese of Texas clergy and staff at Camp Allen, Texas; and to students in the Lay School of Theology and the Certificate Program at the Episcopal Theological Seminary of the Southwest.

I owe thanks to all of those I've mentioned above and to others I'm afraid I haven't, with the customary understanding that any egregious errors in fact, interpretation, or spelling are mine alone.

Finally, I owe especial thanks to Ghost Ranch in Abiquiu, New Mexico, where this book was conceived and written. Jim Baird was my host and patron, again. Gracias, mi amigo. I'm also thankful to Edgar Davy and the staff of the wonderful Ghost Ranch library, just about my favorite place on earth to do research and writing for a book of this kind.

And so I release these words to the winds. My prayer is that this book will spark your thoughts into flame, and that God will richly bless you in your own quest for truth and understanding.

Introduction

*T*he first time I saw *Pulp Fiction*, in the fall of 1994, I had the feeling that I was watching something miraculous. It wasn't just that I was watching an entertaining and inventive work of art, which the movie certainly was, but as I sat there in the darkened theater, I had a strange and paradoxical thought: I felt that I was in the presence of something holy.

As I watched Quentin Tarantino's violent and often vile film about gangsters, junkies, crooked boxers, armed robbers, and other folks who make up the unpleasant underbelly of the world, I was amazed to discover in each of the film's major stories the light of something I could only call grace, and I was spiritually moved in a way I hadn't been in a church since—well, maybe ever.

When the movie was over, I sat quietly through the closing credits, which is my practice, and then remained seated thinking after the lights came up, which isn't.

To paraphrase Jules (Samuel L. Jackson), one of the film's gangsters: In the words, images, and action of *Pulp Fiction*, I felt the touch of God.

God got involved.

Although the movie made its name in the world as a cleverly written film about gunplay, drug use, profanity, and forced sodomy, what I took away from *Pulp Fiction* was not the violent action, dark humor, and crudity, but embedded themes of grace and redemption and the belief that God was real and powerful. For me, *Pulp Fiction* was a deeply spiritual film, and its use of theological language made it, despite its troublesome content, deeply religious as well.

About two thirds of the way through the film, for example, when Jules and his colleague Vincent (John Travolta) survive an attack at point-blank gunpoint, he rejects Vincent's judgment that they were simply lucky. No, he says:

> **Jules:** That was . . . divine intervention. You know what divine intervention is?
>
> **Vincent:** Yeah, I think so. That means God came down from Heaven and stopped the bullets.
>
> **Jules:** Yeah, man, that's what it means. That's exactly what it means! God came down from Heaven and stopped the bullets.[1]

Whether Quentin Tarantino, the writer and director of this scene, believes that God came down and stopped the bullets is irrelevant. Despite Vincent's skepticism, Jules does believe it, and the filmed scene creates an undeniable effect of awe and mystery. Jules is a character we like and respect, and his belief in the miraculous ultimately spills over onto the audience. Whatever Tarantino's own take on the action, this is one of many spots in *Pulp Fiction* that offers us what Connie Neal, author of *The Gospel according to Harry Potter,* likes to call "glimmers of the gospel," moments in popular culture narratives where we can find inspiration and spiritual illumination.[2]

As we'll see in later chapters, *Pulp Fiction* is crammed full of these moments that illuminate Judeo-Christian teachings, whether in its story of Jules's redemption, its account of Vincent first receiving the wages of sin and then experiencing a miraculous second birth, its depiction of people behaving with uncharacteristic kindness and generosity in difficult situations, or its use of an actual vehicle called "Grace" to convey some of its characters to a new life.

The first time I saw *Pulp Fiction*, I noticed some of these things, but I had no idea then that the movie would be discussed in books on the Bible and film, film and spirituality, or even film and prayer. I didn't know that people were going to spend thousands of hours on the Internet and in coffee shops debating such topics as whether

the briefcase Jules and Vincent had rescued contained the soul of
Marcellus Wallace, the gang boss played by Ving Rhames. I didn't
know that I'd actually be opening my dust-covered King James
Bible for the first time in years to read Ezekiel 25:17 and see how
much of that verse Jules was actually quoting to the people he was
getting ready to ventilate. And I didn't know that the venerable
American Academy of Religion, this country's foremost organiza-
tion of theologians and religious scholars, would devote a special
session of their next annual conference to the discussion of *Pulp
Fiction*.

All I knew was that when I left the theater, it was as a slightly
different person than I was when I went in—slightly more hopeful, slightly more open to the possibility that there might be a God
(and to the possibility that he, she, or it might be moving in my
life), and more than a little anxious to have that kind of experience
with the holy again. When Jules discusses the miracle they witnessed ("*You* witnessed," the skeptical Vince says; "I witnessed a
freak occurrence"), he uses those words I mentioned earlier, words
I've co-opted over and over in the intervening years to explain the
feeling I have gotten from *Pulp Fiction*, and from other works of
popular culture that didn't set out to witness to the gospel but do
so anyway: "What is significant is I felt God's touch."

I ultimately saw *Pulp Fiction* in the theater seven times, six
times in the States, once in London. I bought the movie, first on
videocassette and then on DVD, read and reread the screenplay.
Pulp Fiction became a touchstone in my growing faith, more
meaningful than most sermons I'd heard and most church services
I'd sat through. Like many in church and even more outside it, I
have found that God can sometimes speak to me as powerfully
through elements of the culture as through a formal religious service or in a religious setting.

I've learned lessons about my faith and about my life through the
depiction of joy and beauty in musicals like *Top Hat* and *Singin' in
the Rain*, by witnessing a selfless messiah figure and a redeemed
Barabbas in *Casablanca*, in the complicated interplay of guilt and
justice in *Rear Window*, by following the chilling progress of a man
losing his soul in *The Godfather*, in the paradigm of irrational and

unshakable faith put into action in *Close Encounters of the Third Kind*, through the meditations on sin and violence in *Unforgiven*, in the sacrificial love displayed in *Titanic*, and in the scenes of divine intervention and inspired forgiveness that animate Paul Thomas Anderson's *Magnolia*. As this book shows, my spiritual journey has been marked by many cinematic rest stops, and I'm hardly alone in this.

When Chris Seay and I wrote *The Gospel Reloaded* about the religious elements in the *Matrix* films, we were partly inspired to do so because of a thousand Web sites and who knows how many people on the Web discussing faith and philosophy in the original *Matrix*, a phenomenon unseen, perhaps, since the first *Star Wars* films. Many of those people so interested in learning what kind of savior Neo (Keanu Reeves) was and how biblical references helped explain the film's conflict were "irreligious" or "unchurched," to use some religious catchphrases. But every human being is a spiritual being, and we all thirst for something beyond ourselves, however and wherever we can find it, and that book and others like it served a real and growing need.

These days, almost every mainline Protestant church with sufficient resources seems to do "popcorn theology" nights and teach classes on faith and film. In the past five years, secular and religious publishers alike have sent forth books examining the relationship between movies and faith, and popular Web sites like Hollywood Jesus and media sources like the radio shows hosted by Dick Staub and Bill Hogg likewise focus on the intersection of popular culture and Christianity. And in what would have seemed amazing twenty years ago when most of their energy might have gone toward condemning movies from the pulpit and the podium, today leaders in many emerging churches show Hollywood films during sermons and use them in video installations, and universities and seminaries alike offer wildly popular courses on film and theology.

Not everyone is jumping on board this fast-accelerating bandwagon, of course. While *Pulp Fiction* is a movie that was an essential part of the faith journey for me and for many others, it's important to note that a vast number of Americans consider this movie not only un-Christian but sinful, both in itself and as the potential occasion of sin in others. The Office for Film and Broadcasting of the U.S. Conference of Catholic Bishops, which rates films for the millions of American Catholics, actually condemned *Pulp Fiction* as "morally offensive" when it came out in 1994, thus making it off-limits for good Catholics to view.

In fact, the Office for Film and Broadcasting has given their condemnatory rating of "morally offensive" to a number of films that I've discussed with audiences in churches, universities, youth camps, and seminaries for their moral and religious content, among them *American Beauty, Dogma, Kill Bill,* and the Oscar-winning *Million Dollar Baby,* which I have taught fruitfully for its main character's active engagement with God, but which the Office for Film and Broadcasting condemns as a "somber meditation on assisted suicide with a morally problematic ending."[3]

This review points out a central distinction between what this book attempts and what some Christians seem to expect from Hollywood: while every year Hollywood releases movies than can fruitfully illuminate the life of faith and draw us closer to the divine, very very few commercial movies are ever intended as some sort of religious experience. They're stories, some better told than others, and many of them are going to lack an easy moral or be "morally problematic." That's why they require interpretation and our own engagement in the problems they present—*discernment*, to use a good theological word—if we're to gain some sort of enlightenment.

Hollywood films, even in whatever Golden Age people imagine they remember, have always been an uneasy combination of art and commerce, of personal vision and corporate product, and while they can tell mythical stories that touch us deeply, with rare exceptions (like Mel Gibson's *The Passion of the Christ*), our experience of the sacred in a film doesn't come because the filmmakers have consciously devoted themselves to that proposition.

Instead, as my Baylor University colleague Ralph Wood notes in *The Gospel According to Tolkien,* a popular-culture narrative approaches the sacred—if indeed it approaches it at all—through "its plot and characters, its images and tone, its landscape and

point of view—not from any heavy-handed moralizing or preachi-
fying."[4]

That makes for good art but bad evangelism, which is why if
you go to the movies hoping for evangelism, you're almost certain
to be disappointed.

Because of the tension between the surface content of a film and
its possible deeper spiritual meanings, many movies that for me
have strong moral and even religious content are off the shelf for
many Christians, one of the things I hope to remedy with this book.
We Christians do ourselves few favors by refusing to engage the
culture, especially when it regards culture that could help lead a
broken world in the direction of faith and wholeness.

I'll gladly admit that discernment is a necessary element in
approaching popular culture for its sacred content, and movies like
Starship Troopers or *Pootie Tang* may in fact have little or no value
as anything but DVD Frisbees. But if we believe in incarnation—
that is, both the Judeo-Christian belief that God created the world
and the Christian belief that God willingly entered into creation as
a human being—then the world is indeed, as Gerard Manley Hopkins wrote, "charged with the grandeur of God," and with wisdom,
prayer, and persistence we can discern God in the works of God's
creation and in our own creations as well.

The desire to shut ourselves off from parts of the world that
upset or confuse us is understandable, and explains a great deal
about the Christian ark culture that rejects secular culture in favor
of explicitly sacred imitations: Christian romance novels, Christian thrash metal, Christian breath mints. But theologian Urban
Holmes argues that a simple black-and-white view of things—
what we'll discover is traditionally called a Manichean view of the
universe, that spirit is always good and matter is always evil—fails
to take into account that in a world that God has entered, "if we
defend ourselves from everything, we shut out God."[5] That's why
I argue for the serious study of spiritual messages in popular culture from both a narrative point of view and a theological point of
view: I do not want to miss out on any possibility that God may be
speaking to me.

As persuasive as I hope to be in these pages, I know that there

will still be people who'll disagree with the entire premise of this
book, and I do have sympathy for that viewpoint. Almost from the
moment that the movie business relocated from the East Coast to
Hollywood, moralists have pointed a pained finger at the hedonis-
tic lifestyles of some of the rich and famous in the film community. The content of many films is also both offensive and truly
troubling for a parent, which I am, and for a person of faith, which
I likewise am. You may be sure that I'm very careful what movies
I let my eight-year-old see, and many of the films I argue passion-
ately for in this book he will not see until he is much, much older,
if ever. But I don't think it's fair to say that no one else should see
those films because they're not appropriate for him, and I think the
same goes for films I might find offensive that are somehow meaningful to you. The Jewish author and poet Rodger Kamenetz often
talks about how we are drawn to the stories that we need to hear to
be healed. What you need to hear may be very different from what
I need, and yet both of our healing stories may come from God.

In talking about where our sacred stories come from, I could
also argue, of course, that even the Bible, the central source of faith
and religious authority for most Christians, is the product of bad
role models—Moses, who was a murderer and a chronic com-
plainer, is reputed to have written the first five books of the Hebrew
Scriptures; David, the psalmist, was a savage warrior, an adulterer,
and a really rotten parent; and those bickering nitwit disciples of
Jesus credited by some people with creations such as the books of
Matthew, Mark, Peter, and the Revelation?

Don't even get me started on that.

I could also argue that the Bible contains more disturbing subject matter than any five R-rated movies: those bickering patriarchs
and matriarchs in Genesis, whose lust-filled dysfunctional families
make the ones in *Peyton Place*, *East of Eden*, *Home for the Holidays*, or *One True Thing* look like the Brady Bunch; that desperate
housewife Jael who hammers a nail through the skull of an enemy
general in a cold-blooded murder described for us in excruciating
slow-motion; and there's that appalling episode in the book of
Judges where a crowd of men in the city of Gibeah wants to gang-
rape a Levite, a holy man, and so to protect himself he shoves his

mistress into the street so that they can rape and beat her instead, and after he collects her dead body the next morning, he cuts her into pieces (Seriously! Look it up!) and sends messengers bearing the pieces of her mutilated carcass to each tribe of Israel to protest the way he (he!) was dishonored by the people of Gibeah.[6]

Folks, *Pulp Fiction* and *Sin City* have nothing on these stories from the Bible.

Still and all, that's not the point, is it? It's not the character of the writers of the Bible—or the negative faith example that many of these disgusting stories in the Bible provide—that we remember, nor should we remember them. No one has ever suggested in my hearing that the Levite in Judges, for example, is a role model, even though his story is in the Bible and many Christians believe that each word in there is inspired by God to show us how to live. If we really want to grow in faith and learn how to live, then obviously we should internalize the positive stories and put aside the ones that degrade our spirits and teach us nothing but selfishness, violence, or faithlessness.

The same is true for popular culture. If something feels bad, then don't do it, and for goodness sake, don't let your kids do it. But in a world full of people who are starved for faith and connection to the divine wherever they can find it, Hollywood films can be a vital link on the way to or as a part of a spiritual life, just as they were for me.

The fact is, as disturbing as some might find this, the number of Americans watching movies every week far outnumbers the number of people showing up at church, synagogue, madrassa, or ashram. Although many more people watch movies at home these days than at the theaters, which comparative anthropologist Joseph Campbell once called contemporary "temples," we still approach movies with a sense of ritual, and they still constitute a powerful shared myth that we talk about, whether in real time or in virtual time.[7]

If indeed "movies have always been a religious experience," as Jack Foley, of Focus Pictures, argues, my continuing argument will be that if we can show the spiritually hungry a connection between the popular forms of narrative they religiously consume and our own core faith narratives, then I certainly think we ought to try.[8] Brian McLaren, a pastor and storyteller who has long preached an annual series on "God in the Movies" because he sees moments of "glory" in films, writes of the current age, "Before us lies a new world—a world nearly empty spiritually, which makes it hungry and thirsty for good spiritual bread and wine. It is a world hostile to dogmatism but ready to be sown with good seeds of vibrant, living faith. If we as Christians do not fill the need, someone else will."[9]

Feeding the hungry and thirsty is indeed what I hope we'll be doing in this book.

In chapter 1, we'll examine how Hollywood films can shed an angle of light on the most basic proposition of Judeo-Christian theology, the existence of God. We'll see how stories of the supernatural like *It's a Wonderful Life*, *Field of Dreams*, and more "realistic" films like *American Beauty* and *Magnolia* all contain moving evidence of the divine presence. In the films of two cinematic masters, Alfred Hitchcock and N. Night Shyamalan, we'll explore how the explicit presence of the artist behind the camera can suggest to us the presence of the creator of our own reality.

In chapter 2, we'll see how movies have presented valuable images of God that can help explain the way God is and works in the world and in our lives. Building out from the essential Christian notion of a Trinitarian God—one God who consists of three persons, Father, Son, and Holy Spirit—we'll see how *To Kill a Mockingbird*, *Cool Hand Luke*, *The Matrix*, and other films might dramatically demonstrate the interworkings of the Trinity, and how movies have presented characters who can represent for us each of the distinct persons of the Godhead: Father/Creator, Son/Redeemer, and Spirit/Sustainer.

In chapter 3, we'll explore what Hollywood films can tell us about sin and evil. Christians believe that God sent Jesus into a world full of hurting and broken people, whose sin had separated them from the love of God and from each other, to rescue us and to restore wholeness and communion. We'll take a look at Hollywood versions of a fallen world—what Augustine called the "Earthly City"—in the classic *film noir Double Indemnity*, explore the traditional supernatural genesis of sin in *The Lord of the Rings* and Harry Potter films, and discover the human manifestations of evil in films like *Schindler's List* and *Munich*.

In chapter 4, we'll talk about the concept of redemption, how some of the American films we've discussed present powerful secular versions of the religious conversion and change that Christians believe to be central to salvation. We'll trace the change in self-centered characters in *The Philadelphia Story, North by Northwest, The Fisher King*, and other films, and conclude with a discussion of how Hollywood love stories can teach us essential truths about redemption.

In chapter 5, we'll ask what converted people should be doing with their lives and suggest that they should work to bring the values of peace and justice into a world that desperately needs healing and wholeness. We'll look at films like *Robin Hood, Brokeback Mountain*, and *Crash* that can teach us how Christians should pursue economic justice and fight prejudice, and *Paths of Glory* and *Unforgiven* to show how violence and war should never be Christian solutions.

In chapter 6, we'll look at the depictions of the church and contemporary Christian belief in the movies, and we'll close with a discussion of what I perceive as a growing openness toward faith stories in our culture. Instead of segregating faith in period costume dramas about Jesus, Moses, or Noah's ark, contemporary Hollywood films, even some made by hip un-Christian filmmakers, often contain a strong spiritual or religious element. Faith is no longer a taboo subject in American popular culture. We'll examine how American films—including Christmas films—demonstrate the hunger for faith, and consider what that new openness toward spirituality might mean for the future of American movies. Throughout this book, unattributed quotations are drawn from the films themselves. Screenplays are useful for gauging a writer's original intentions, although they may (as here) differ from the completed film.

So that's what's happening in this book. I want to offer you a learned yet accessible look at films that can inspire as well as entertain, to show how you might use these films to discuss theological issues, and, wherever possible, to tie the stories of these films back to our core narratives about salvation and the life of faith.

I love movies for lots of reasons—I love the action, the sweep of the big screen, the feeling of being immersed in a story, the exotic worlds they show us.

But it wasn't the action, the big screen, or being immersed in a life of crime that inspired me to pay full admission for *Pulp Fiction* seven times.

It was the startling and moving depiction of the life of faith.

And that's what I hope you'll find within these pages as well: movie moments that will startle and move you toward God.

Chapter One

Faith and Belief

Does God Exist?

God and Creation

About two years ago, my screenwriter friend Derek Haas (*2 Fast 2 Furious*, *Catch That Kid*, and others) took me wandering across the deserted Warner Brothers studio back lot in Burbank, California. As I looked around, I saw familiar sunlit streets and movie sets, and poked my head into cavernous empty soundstages where movies from *Casablanca* to *Batman* have been filmed. At one time, giants walked this earth: Humphrey Bogart and Bette Davis, Gary Cooper and Cary Grant, Superman and Batman. But now, since it was May and most of the TV shows that shot at Warner Brothers were on hiatus, we were virtually alone as we walked past an outdoor set for *ER* and poked our heads into a stage where *The West Wing* is filmed, moving from abandoned world to abandoned world.

I knew that even though I couldn't see it reflected in the present moment, each of these wondrous little worlds was built for (and perhaps, by) a powerful entity—a director, a producer, these days, of course, maybe even on behalf of a petulant actor—who presided over a miniature reality like a miniature God.

Hollywood history gives us plenty of examples of autocratic producers like David O. Selznick (*Gone with the Wind*) and directors like Cecil B. DeMille (*The Ten Commandments*), who lorded it over the people on their sets. On their sets, you never had to wonder if they existed: just stand still long enough and

1

you'd hear people talking about one of those voluminous amphetamine-fueled memos from Selznick that almost carried the power of the divine, or perhaps hear DeMille imperiously say (as indeed, he did say), "You are here to please me. Nothing else on earth matters."

But as I walked the sets with Derek, we were a long way away from Selznick and DeMille and their modern counterparts, and all that we were left with was the realities they—or someone—created.

But the artificial worlds of the movie set—and also of the created movie, as we will see—present useful models for exploring the existence of God. Clearly someone somewhere put these things into place on the set, even if he, she, or it isn't currently calling "Action!" and "Cut!" and even if we can't see whoever's in charge moving the people and the scenery around for best dramatic effect.

It makes me wonder if screenwriter Andrew Niccol came up with the idea for *The Truman Show* after a similar experience of walking the back lot. His story of a powerful producer/director, the aptly named Christof (Ed Harris), who presides over the ultimate reality show—a stage set where a man named Truman Burbank (Jim Carrey) has literally spent his life under Christof's watchful eyes—could be, in one sense, a story of our own lives lived out under the eyes of a powerful creator God in a creation placed here for our use and enjoyment. Gradually, as Truman begins to seek the truth, he sees the flickers behind the scenes and becomes aware that Christof created and runs his world, and Christof reveals himself to Truman (and to us) from his vault (okay, his office) in the heavens (okay, the ceiling) where he looks down on the vast set he's built for Truman to experience.

Since Cristof is only human, he's a less-than-satisfactory God for all his power and creativity. But there are aspects of Cristof's character that can help us understand elements of the real God. Christof has power, of a kind, to make things happen, and he chooses to use it in creating a world—a world designed to get huge TV ratings for the network, true, but a world nonetheless. He watches over Truman as though acting out the words of the old gospel hymn:

His eye is on the sparrow
And I know he watches me.

And although Cristof is an inscrutable character, he seems to care for Truman, even though his actions don't always demonstrate that. *The Truman Show* dramatically illustrates a question about God that has been a puzzle for theologians and believers alike, one that ultimately, as H. Richard Niebuhr writes, can only be approached as an item of belief: "Given: God is faithful, even if we cannot understand the mode of his faithfulness."[1] Although, as we'll see in chapter 2, God has appeared in Scripture in various guises, some of which have been frightening or difficult to fathom, one of the givens that Christians have chosen to accept is that God is benevolent and takes an interest in us, fulfilling, as the famous prayer from Chrysostom says, our desires and petitions as may be best for us. As we will see later, we may be challenged by events that seem to suggest God doesn't take this benevolent approach to us, and sometimes we may wonder, indeed, if God cares for us at all. But ultimately this has to be a matter of faith, and perhaps a matter of choice. As Archbishop Rowan Williams puts it, one has "no temptation to model one's behaviour on a God utterly without any investment in the life of creation."[2] Cristof, whatever his quirks, has a real, if personal, interest in preserving the happiness of Truman, his creation.

The Truman Show is thus one of a number of Hollywood movies that suggests to us that whether we can perceive it or not, there is an order at the heart of creation, a presence beyond our perception, and these films direct us to consider the questions, Is there a God? And if so, what sort of God? By talking about some movies that suggest divine mechanisms behind the curtain of our reality or that take seeking, belief, or faith in a higher power as their subjects, we can see how they can be useful for us in our own seeking. By considering the filmmaking of Alfred Hitchcock and M. Night Shyamalan as models for an interaction between creator and creation that proves the reality of both, we can see a vision of the creator God we have begun to examine here. All of this will lead us then in chapter 2 to consider other images of God we find in film and to ask how they might bring us to a greater understanding of the divine.

So far we have defined God largely in terms of the act of creation, but of course a definition of what God is and does could fill volumes (and in the hands of some theologians, has). Traditional Christian belief suggests that God created us, sustains us, and offers us the opportunity to become, somehow, one with the divine when our earthly lives are ended. What else might we say about God? Anselm wrote that God was that being or force or power greater than which nothing could be conceived to exist.[3] This perfect being created everything that is, and is itself essential being, as Thomas Aquinas puts it. Created beings might in some sense resemble God, but God does not resemble created beings.[4] So we might begin our cinematic search for divinity by saying that God is, then, both all-powerful and benign, the fount of all existence and the source of our being, something or someone in whose image we are made but not made in ours, and perhaps beyond our understanding except with God's own assistance.

That has never prevented us from trying to understand, of course, and despite our recognition that God is not human, we still tend to imagine God in our own image since it's next to impossible to get outside our own experience. That's why we look up at the big screen to find some finite human portraying that which nothing can be greater than, essential being: George Burns is God (*Oh God I* and *II*), or Morgan Freeman or Jim Carrey (*Bruce Almighty*), or Alanis Morissette (*Dogma*). Again, it's hardly surprising, even though we know it's inaccurate; we have a long human heritage of imagining God as somehow human. The Bible anthropomorphizes God constantly: God lays his hand upon Egypt in Exodus 7, snorts or flares his nostrils in 2 Samuel 22:9 (the Hebrew word can be translated as both "anger" and "nose," and probably is intended to be translated both ways), and in Exodus 33:23, Moses sees the divine backside ("back parts" is how the King James Version has it) since no human can see God's face and live.

But we can find plenty of movies that suggest we live in a reality created by a benign and all-powerful being without even mentioning *Oh God!* (We will, in fact, never mention it again.) Films that feature supernatural characters like angels and devils from our sacred stories, films that depict the presence of miracles, and films that display a recognition of the beauty and order of creation all create cinematic realities that can express the reality of God. In these films, sometimes God is a tangible presence or even a character, sometimes God is a power or presence perceived only through the events of the story, and sometimes God is the sort of unmoved mover that Aristotle imagined might be at the heart of all things. But all of these films turn our eyes beyond this reality to what might lie beyond and above it, and in doing so inspire us to believe.

The Supernatural as Proofs of God

As we mentioned, films featuring angels (or devils) automatically turn our God detectors on. The *Anchor Bible Dictionary* succinctly notes that angels are "heavenly beings whose function it is to serve God and to execute God's will."[5] In both scriptural and extra-scriptural Jewish, Christian, and Muslim sacred narratives, angels serve as God's messengers and assistants: angels bring the Virgin Mary news that she will bear God's son, reveal God's instructions to the patriarchs and word to the prophets, and even, as in the story of Balaam the prophet in chapter 22 of Numbers, scare the wits out of poor donkeys. Given these associations, the presence of angels automatically opens the door of our consciousness to the divine, which may explain why and how angel-mania has bombarded American culture in recent years with images, stories, and TV shows like *Touched by an Angel.* Angelology is a way of talking about God without having to talk about God. If you believe in angels, then you have to acknowledge the One who sent them.

It's unfortunate, then, that so many movies featuring angels are so barely worth watching. *Michael,* for example, in which the title archangel is played with lusty burping gusto by John Travolta, is about as bad as angel movies can get, suggesting that angels (even archangels, the upper management of the angelic host) have nothing better to do than hang around honkytonks and resurrect dead pets. When we consider that in Christian tradition Michael was imagined to be Satan's angelic foe, then the film makes us ask whether Satan no longer needs a whipping, or whether God has just given up.

The Bishop's Wife stars Cary Grant as a suave angel come to convince Loretta Young that her pious clergyman of a husband (played by David Niven) is still worth loving and supporting (and confusing her to no end, since, of course, he is simultaneously a supernatural messenger from God and hunky Cary Grant), but while the movie is as charming as Michael is not, viewers might rightfully feel a little strange about the implied attraction between spiritual being and human being and might also rightfully ask, in a nation that today suffers from rampant divorce, is the bishop's work for the Lord so important that he somehow merits divine intervention in his marital life? (The same sorts of questions about guardian angels attain in City of Angels, an American remake of the vastly superior Wim Winders film Wings of Desire. Roger Ebert chalks it up to our selfish spiritual desire to believe we're all important enough to merit this kind of divine intervention, and as for this queasy cross-species love story, he says that Hollywood tends mostly to have an interest in spiritual creatures when they become carnal, "in priests and nuns when they break the vow of chastity, and with angels only when they get the hots for humans.")[6]

More recently, the movie Constantine depicted a cosmic battle between good and evil in which the archangel Gabriel (Tilda Swinton) plays (finally) a role that doesn't require falling in love with a human. Theologically speaking, we might call Gabriel's a more traditional angelic role, although it is revealed, ultimately, as misguided. She/he has long served as an intermediary for God on the front lines of a cosmic battle involving angels and devils that many of us remember (we think) from John Milton's Paradise Lost, but at last Gabriel takes a little too much individual initiative in testing humanity. Since Gabriel says that humans only rise to their best natures in the face of great adversity, she/he wants to bring on an apocalyptic calamity that will make humans act in a way truly worthy of God's love and forgiveness. Occultist John Constantine

(Keanu Reeves) just manages to avert this calamity by last-minute negotiations with Satan (Peter Stormare) himself.

The presence of demons and devils (and especially a personified Satan) in *Constantine* and other films is another supernatural watermark on a reality that has a God even if God is never specifically mentioned. The apocryphal Hebrew books of Enoch are a primary source for our cosmology of angels and devils, and clearly the writers of *Constantine*, the film (and *Hellblazer*, the comic book on which it is based), have some knowledge of this tradition. Devils, the books of Enoch tell us, were once angels, but they rebelled against God and were cast out of heaven. Early Christian fathers like Irenaeus and Justin Martyr referred to this war in heaven in their writings and made it a respectable part of Christian lore, and later, the literary works of John Milton and William Blake made the angelic rebellion an artistic truth.

When Satan appears at the end of *Constantine* in all his slimy glory, he speaks of the contest with his adversary, God, in which John Constantine has found himself embroiled. Films in which Satan or his future ally (at least, according to the book of Revelation), the antichrist, appear also direct our attention toward God, whether or not God's name is ever mentioned. If you have an adversary, you have to have a God he opposes, and if you have an antichrist, well, you have to have a Christ.

Unfortunately, again, as with movies about angels, most films in which Satan, the antichrist, or generic devils appear strain a viewer's patience. But films like *Rosemary's Baby*, *The Exorcist*, and *The Omen* both chill us with their visions of ultimate evil and suggest that somewhere there must be a counterpart of ultimate good. Consider the case of *Hellboy*, derived, like *Constantine*, from a highly acclaimed comic book. Although the villain, Rasputin (Karel Roden), says at one point, "Your God chooses to remain silent," the film is not at all silent about the existence of God. It is, first, chock-full of religious images, architecture, and objects: crosses, rosaries, ruined abbeys, relics like the spear that pierced the side of Christ, salt gathered from the tears of a thousand angels. And, oh yes, a bunch of demons and the Beast of the Apocalypse.

It turns out that Hellboy (Ron Perlman, painted a bright red) was brought to earth as a baby demon by the resurrected Rasputin when he was collaborating with the Nazis on something called the Ragnarok Project toward the end of World War II. Ragnarok is the Norse myth concerning the end of the world, and Hellboy's destiny, Rasputin tells him, is to usher in that destruction. In a flashfoward, Rasputin shows Professor Bruttenholm (John Hurt), Hellboy's human adoptive father, a vision of that future—Hellboy with a burning crown of fire hovering atop his head, a flapping newpaper with the headline "The Apocalypse," and a world of blasted skyscrapers that looks as though nuclear devastation has fallen across the length and breadth of it.

Rasputin has said that God chooses to remain silent. Yet at the movie's climax, when Hellboy stands at the brink of realizing his satanic destiny and ushering in the end of the world, his adoptive father's crucifix burns a clearly identifiable cross into his palm, a sign that stops him in his tracks and helps him to choose against both his destiny and his nature. He snaps the demonic horns from his forehead and instead of destroying the world, destroys Rasputin.

That glowing image of the cross is a powerful lesson that with God on our side, anything is possible.

It's also a reminder to us that where there are miracles in the movies, God is present, even if God seems to remain silent.

It's a Miracle!

Miracles, angels, and a cameo by God himself make *It's a Wonderful Life* not just the quintessential Christmas movie, but also a vital movie proposing the existence of God. One of the major characters in the film, of course, is a slightly befuddled angel-in-training named Clarence Oddbody. As we've noted of angels, Clarence's presence would alert us to the possibility that this movie will take God's existence as a necessary given, but the movie gives us much more evidence than one fumbling angel.

At the beginning of the movie, we are actually introduced to the character "God," who, while he appears here as a twinkling star who speaks, is directly involved in the events of the movie (and presumably, of the world) through observation and the intervention of divine agents such as Clarence. This is clearly a God who cares, the benign creator we've been talking about, and it is a fortunate thing, since this is a story in which divine intervention may be the only thing that stops a good man from destroying himself in despair.

In the dark days of the Great Depression, George Bailey (Jimmy Stewart) faces a crisis of faith—in himself, in humanity, and ultimately, in God—because the savings and loan to which he's unwillingly given his life in the town of Bedford Falls has failed. Even worse, it has been destroyed by Potter, the town banker, a vile capitalist if ever there was one. Ruined and disgraced, George is ready to end it all until, as most breathing Americans know, Clarence the angel drops in to show him what his town would have been like if George hadn't been around.

What follows is a nightmare vision—almost a hell on earth—but because he's able to see what Bedford Falls would look like as Pottersville, George ultimately wants to live again, and when more miraculous events put things right at the end of the movie, perhaps he will finally lose his deep-seated discontent that his life hadn't turned out as he'd wanted.

What makes these miracles possible? Well, pretty clearly it is divine intervention that comes about because of a multitude of prayers headed God-ward. Immediately following the opening credits and two establishing shots of Bedford Falls, the film's action begins with six shots of buildings accompanied by voice-over narration. Issuing from every edifice are prayers for George Bailey:

Mr. Gower: I owe everything to George Bailey. Help him, dear father.

Martini: Joseph, Jesus, and Mary, help my friend Mr. Bailey.

George's Mother: Help my son George tonight.

> **Bert:** He never thinks about himself, God; that's why he's in trouble.
>
> **Ernie:** George is a good guy, give him a break, God.

And finally, at George's house, we hear the voices of his wife and daughter:

> **Mary:** Dear Lord, watch over him tonight.
>
> **Zuzu:** Please God, something's the matter with Daddy. Please bring Daddy back. Please bring Daddy home.

Is there a God who hears? You bet there is. These prayers prompt an immediate divine response: the camera tilts upward from these shots of buildings to the heavens, and that's when we hear the voices of God and Chief Angel Joseph (and see them as twinkling stars) as they summon Clarence and put him on the job.

Another prayer is heard in this movie, as well—George's prayer, delivered out of the very depths of despair:

> **George:** God, dear Father in Heaven, I'm not a praying man, but if you're up there and you can hear me, show me the way. I'm at the end of my rope. Show me the way.

At first it doesn't seem as though George's prayer will be answered. But we've seen from the beginning of the film that God is up there; God does hear. And in *It's a Wonderful Life*, God does indeed work to show George the way.

God does not twinkle like a star in *Field of Dreams*, a similar movie released four decades later, but it too is a movie full of miracles that make us wonder where they might come from; its star Kevin Costner in fact called it "Our generation's *It's a Wonderful Life*."[7] Although neither W. P. Kinsella, who wrote *Shoeless Joe*, the novel the movie was based on, nor writer/director Phil Alden Robinson would describe themselves as believers in the supernatural, they created a story that knits together life after death, the granting of wishes, the reconciliation of a son with his dead father, and, ultimately, a visit to heaven. And if indeed in this movie we can't see God twinkling above, perhaps we might imagine we hear God below.

Field of Dreams was advertised in theaters by a preview that opened with the words "First came the voice" emblazoned across the screen. You don't have to know much Bible to recognize an echo of the first verse of the Gospel of John. "In the beginning was the Word," is the familiar rendering from the King James Version, "and the Word was with God, and the Word was God," while a contemporary translation of John actually begins, "In the beginning, the Voice was speaking."[8] What is this voice? Well, we can say that it calls out to a simple farmer, Ray Kinsella (Costner), in his cornfield and asks him to do something ridiculous, impossible. But when the farmer listens—and obeys—he is rewarded by being a witness to miracles.

It's a familiar story: Moses was a sheepherder when a burning bush caught his eye and a voice came forth and told him he was going to confront the Egyptian pharaoh, perhaps the most powerful man in the world, with nothing more than his sandals and a wooden staff. David was a shepherd, too, and just a boy when Samuel, the prophet of the Lord, told him he was going to be king of Israel. The Bible is full of ridiculous calls to adventure that ultimately prove to be inspired, and *Field of Dreams* is no different in the way Ray Kinsella is called.

"The Voice," incidentally, is listed in the film's closing credits as being played by "Himself," which calls to mind God's naming of himself in Exodus 3:14: "I AM WHO I AM." "Himself" first urges Ray to plow under his cornfield and build a baseball field, then to drive to Boston to contact a reclusive writer, and finally to locate an unknown baseball player who never got the chance to bat in the major leagues. These tasks or trials come against the backdrop of the same sort of impending financial ruin that brought George Bailey to the brink of suicide, but Ray never breaks faith with the voice because a series of miracles convince him that there must be a beneficent order to his universe that he simply can't see yet.

These are, after all, good-sized miracles: for starters, the great Shoeless Joe Jackson (Ray Liotta) returns from the dead to play baseball on the field Ray built, then he brings others from somewhere out in the cornfield to join him. Ray convinces the reclusive writer Terence Mann (James Earl Jones) to make a trek to Minnesota, and they bring the long-dead Doc "Moonlight" Graham (Burt Lancaster) his chance to hit against a major-league pitcher. And at the end of the movie, when it looks as though the world will collapse into disaster just as George Bailey's world almost did, more miracles, fast as popping corn: Doc Graham steps back across the foul line to save the life of Ray's daughter, Terry Mann gets a chance to go with the ballplayers "out there" into the cornfield, Ray's long-dead father, who had been a minor-league ballplayer, takes off his catcher's mask and stands looking at Ray from the backstop, and off in the distance a line of cars receding to the horizon has shown up to visit this field of dreams—and to pay enough per head, we presume, so that Ray will be able to keep the farm.

On paper it all looks slightly ridiculous, and indeed Phil Alden Robinson's script bounced around Hollywood for years. People were afraid to make such a fantastic movie because they didn't believe audiences would accept it. But as a story and as an experience, Costner's evaluation of the movie is right on: like *It's a Wonderful Life*, *Field of Dreams* makes you believe that these miracles can happen.

And more, that they should happen.

Now, where do the miracles come from? Twice characters ask Ray the question "Is this heaven?" Both times he answers them in the negative—"No, this is Iowa"—but the literary device of repetition calls that answer into question even before Ray's exchange with his father at the end of the film:

> **Ray:** Is there a heaven?
>
> **John:** Oh yeah. It's the place where dreams come true.

Ray looks at his father, miraculously returned to him in the prime of life like the other ballplayers, as though they were raised into the spiritual bodies the apostle Paul talked about in 1 Corinthians 15. He looks around at the lush green baseball field he has built against everyone's best advice, at the beautiful summer evening, at his wife and newly rescued daughter on the front porch of his farmhouse, and he has an epiphany. "Maybe this *is* heaven," he says.

Heaven is where dreams come true. But heaven is also where God is. Although the how and why of the miracles is never spelled out—certainly no one in this movie prays for God to intervene on Ray's behalf—we can't escape the conclusion that some benign presence in the cosmos has intervened to set things right in the lives of all of these characters and to reconcile what has gone wrong, if not in this life, in the life to come. And who do we imagine has the power to do that, control over life and death, and the desire to see reconciliation and redemption if not God?

Miracles—divine interventions, if you will—puzzle us. We may believe they come from God, and so there must be a God, but we don't know how and we don't know why the miracles come. Take, for example, Vincent and Jules, the hit men played by John Travolta and Samuel L. Jackson in *Pulp Fiction*. As we saw in the introduction, when a junior gangster empties his gun at Vincent and Jules at point-blank range and they aren't even nicked, Jules takes this to be divine intervention, a miracle of God, and he determines to change his life for the better, starting now. If there's a God up there, he does not want to be a bad guy anymore.

As they're sitting at breakfast following their stressful morning, Jules asks the still skeptical Vincent if he knows what a miracle is.

Sure, Vincent says, with his mouth full: It's an act of God. And when Jules presses him, he says that he supposes a miracle happens when God makes the impossible possible. This is indeed how we're used to thinking of miracles, as big and splashy, and certainly the film miracles we've discussed up to now have been that sort: God sends an angel down to stop a potential suicide, long-dead ballplayers show up on your front lawn—those are hard to ignore. But as Jules tells Vincent, miracles come in all shapes and sizes, and they don't necessarily have to be big and splashy. In fact, they don't even have to be God making the impossible possible.

God in the Everyday

One of my favorite novels, Willa Cather's *Death Comes for the Archbishop,* contains a passage where two Catholic priests discuss miracles. One likes them big and splashy, the miracle as sign, old school, the way Jesus used to do them. The other wonders if perhaps what happens in a miracle is not God working against the normal fabric of the universe, but our perception being broadened enough so that we can suddenly see something that has been there all along, the fabulous weave and warp of the universe revealed.[9]

In the Age of the Enlightenment, when Isaac Newton and other worthies were using science to uncover the weave and warp of the universe, a popular view of the cosmos was that of God as divine clock maker. Some Deists thought of God as having created and wound up the clock of the cosmos for all time and then stepped back behind the scenes; others imagined that God needed to rewind the clock every now and again.

Alfred Hitchcock's cameo appearance thirty minutes into his film *Rear Window* is particularly instructive in this context. Hitchcock may be glimpsed for just a moment in a songwriter's apartment, where he is, yes, winding a clock. "Look," Hitch almost seems to be saying in many of his cameos. "You know all of this didn't get here by itself." By stepping out from behind the clockwork for a moment in the films he planned and directed, Hitchcock reminds us that these intricate camera movements, startling camera angles, and expertly edited scenes have both an order and an Orderer. Hitchcock's final cameo in *Family Plot*, fittingly, is as a silhouette behind a door stenciled "Registrar of Births and Deaths."

Now don't get me wrong: I'm a big fan of your big miracle. The scene at the end of Paul Thomas Anderson's *Magnolia* where God sets the world right by sending a shower of falling frogs across the San Fernando Valley is a brilliant example of a big miracle that demonstrates God is up there listening. But films with the second kind of miracle—if we can call the miracle of awareness that—also can show us the presence of God, and since I don't get many big splashy miracles in my everyday life, I discover that I'm also drawn to these quieter moments of revelation. In literary terms, we might call these moments of epiphany ("showing forth"), a sudden intuitive understanding of how the world works, and, just maybe, what is making it work. Gregory of Nyssa suggested that this might in fact be the most suitable proof of God for a person of intellect, even a skeptical one: "If he says God does not exist, then from the skillful and wise arrangement of the world he can be led to acknowledge the existence of some power which is manifested by it and which transcends the universe."[10] A clock winder, if you will.

That's why I love *Magnolia* so much. It doesn't just have a big, splashy, frogs-falling-from-the-sky kind of miracle. It also has an intricate and clearly very intentional pattern of reference to Exodus (the triple repetition of "The sins of the fathers will be visited upon the sons," as indeed they are in this film), and, in particular, Exodus 8:2—the verse in the Hebrew Bible that announces the divine sending of frogs upon Egypt. Scattered throughout the movie from prologue to last scene are eights and twos, often together—a length of hose or rope coiled on a building wall, the number on an airplane, individual cards in a game of blackjack. The sheer volume of eights and twos makes it clear that this is no accident, but the work of the controlling intelligence who created the world of the film. And when we become aware of this pattern, not only are we amazed by the "skillful and wise arrangement" of this world, but I think we also can accept the big miracle with a little more grace.

The movie *American Beauty* contains several such scenes that suggest we live in a universe charged with meaning. Lester Burnham (Kevin Spacey) insists at the beginning and end of the film that there is a pattern and a grand design behind his bizarre and suddenly truncated life, for example, but the most revelatory moments in the film concern Ricky (Wes Bentley), who films everything around him as though he desperately wants to understand it. At one point, in talking about filming a dead subject, Ricky tells Lester's daughter Jane (Thora Birch) that "when you see something like that it's like God is looking right at you, just for a second. And if you're careful, you can look right back."

"And what do you see?" Jane asks.

"Beauty," he says.

These lines are reminiscent of psalms such as Psalm 19:

> The heavens are telling the glory of God;
> and the firmament proclaims his handiwork.[11]

What Ricky is saying is that there is beauty everywhere and that the entire earth testifies to the presence of God within it. This is even more obvious later when Ricky asks Jane if she wants to see "the most beautiful thing I've ever filmed."

It turns out to be a piece of trash caught in a violent wind, one of those white plastic bags that we might use to carry our toothpaste or our milk, blowing around and around in a circle, but as Alan Ball describes it in his screenplay (and director Sam Mendes shoots it) it's every bit as mesmerizing, every bit as beautiful as a white sand beach or a glowing sunset. As we watch the bag circling, swirling, soaring, Ricky is remembering that day aloud, how the bag was almost dancing with him, and how he suddenly understood that "there was this entire life behind things, and this incredibly benevolent force, that wanted me to know there was no reason to be afraid. Ever."

It's an amazing cinematic moment, and a powerful theological moment as well. What Ricky is espousing is a deeply incarnational theology, the belief that God enters into the world and may be seen in it, not just in the majestic heavens but also in the interplay of wind and garbage. Many theologians have argued that nothing in creation is outside the scope of God: The creation myth in the opening chapter of Genesis, of course, shows God looking over his whole creation and finding it all "very good." The Celtic branch of Christianity has long affirmed that "matter matters"; J. Philip Newell summarizes an important and typical strand of Celtic belief by noting that "in the tradition of St. Patrick there is an awareness that all created things carry within them the grace and goodness of God."[12] And Augustine, who is sometimes stereotyped as someone who came to disdain the things of the world, often repeated the Platonic axiom that whatever things exist are good, and concluded after wrestling with the genesis of evil—in what may be the most important conclusion of the *Confessions*—that "it was made clear to me that you made all things good, and there are absolutely no substances which you did not make."[13]

Now Augustine is not affirming that God created Ricky's trash bag; not exactly. But he is suggesting that created matter is inherently good, and that, as Ricky puts it, if you're careful, you can look back through it and see God. John Dominic Crossan suggests that the divine is not just something that occasionally breaks through the surface of the natural world; "it is always there for those with spirit to see and faith to hear."[14]

Some people, as I noted in the introduction, were offended by the bawdy language and sexual subject matter of *American Beauty*, but its screenwriter, Alan Ball, is a devout Christian, and his *Six Feet Under*, which Ball developed for HBO, presented some of the most challenging and moving shows about faith issues ever to appear on television. So don't be surprised if Ricky's language follows us throughout the book. Some people might say that *American Beauty* is as much trash as some floating plastic bag; I see both as proof that there is an incredibly benevolent life behind existence that we can perceive if we're only willing to look through the camera lens.

Signs of God

Ultimately, Christians have affirmed the possibility of both ways of perceiving God that we've discovered in these films, through the big gaudy miracle as well as through our suddenly perceiving a divine order in the world. Aquinas addressed the question of miracles in connection with the implication—unthinkable to many theologians up to this very day—that if God chose to intervene in the world, then God was changing God's mind, or the fragile order of things. And if God changed this order, did that mean that God was changeable? Not at all, Aquinas concluded, citing Augustine. God had created an order, and, at the same time, reserved the right to act outside this order. In other words, miracles were a part of this "ultimate order and plan of creation," even though they might appear to be exceptions to it.[15]

A wondrous example of these two evidences of God—the marvelous everyday and the extraordinary marvel—comes together in

M. Night Shyamalan's *Signs*. Like his previous films, *The Sixth Sense* and *Unbreakable*, *Signs* resonates with a clear sense of the supernatural moving in the world, but the films are also set smack dab in the middle of the here and now and reveal at their conclusion how every seemingly unimportant detail we've witnessed over the last two hours was charged with meaning and part of a creator's plan.

In biblical times, this is typically how signs (or miracles) operated. The Israelites, for example, lived in a world in which people believed their gods had the power to intervene in human history. In New Testament Greek, the word σημεῖα (*semeia*) is typically translated "signs." It might be helpful to think about our own experience with signs, especially on the interstate late at night. When the brightly lit and colored signs draw our attention, they are pointing toward a reality beyond themselves. What's important about them is not themselves (we would not camp out under a Texaco sign and completely ignore the gas pumps) but what they represent: fuel for our cars, food for our bodies, or a good night's sleep.

This is how signs function in the Bible as well. We can be as blinded by the miracles in the Bible as we are by that colorful glow through our windshields, but what the miracles in the Bible typically point to, the object beyond them, is God. Miracles in the Hebrew testament were intended to show God's presence. Moses was given power to aid the Israelites and to demonstrate that God was present; when Joshua took over for Moses, immediately God gave him, too, a parting-the-waters miracle. (The book of Joshua says, "On that day the LORD exalted Joshua in the sight of all Israel; and they stood in awe of him, as they had stood in awe of Moses, all the days of his life.")[16] In the Christian Testament, a skeptical Jewish leader comes to Jesus in the Gospel of John and tells him, "Rabbi, we know that you are a teacher who has come from God; for no one can do these signs that you do apart from the presence of God." Later in John, Jesus laments, "Unless you see signs and wonders you will not believe."[17]

So, in addition to their narrative meaning, signs are intended to point beyond themselves to the existence of God, to make belief possible in a world that looks for signs, and no movie reflects this better than M. Night Shyamalan's *Signs*. *Signs* is simultaneously a science-fiction film, an end-of-the-world thriller, and a family drama. But most importantly, it is a movie about a man, Graham Hess, who is looking for a sign so that he can believe.

The filmmakers themselves make this explicit in their discussion of the movie. Shyamalan says that he and cinematographer Tak Fujimoto conceived of the entire movie as a metaphor (a sign, if you will), "a conversation between God and this one man," and he notes that the title, like most good titles, has multiple layers of meaning. It refers to the elaborate crop circles created as navigation devices by the invading aliens descending from outer space, as well as to "the existence of signs from above in a kind of heavenly manner" for a man who has lost his faith and desperately needs to know that "there's somebody out there" still watching over him.[18]

Why has Graham lost his faith? Six months before the events of the movie, he was an Episcopal priest serving a small town in Pennsylvania. He had the respect of his town, and seems to have been a gentle and reflective soul. I'm guessing he was a good priest. Then one night, his wife was killed in a freak accident when the town veterinarian, Ray Reddy (played by writer/director Shyamalan himself), fell asleep on the drive home and his truck pinned her against a tree. "It's like it was meant to be," Ray tells Graham in what he thinks will be their final conversation, echoing words that Graham's wife said as she was dying.

If you believe in miracles, then it's possible that they can be read as negative as well as positive. Howard Clark Kee points out the different varieties of miracles recorded in the books of the Bible: miracles can confirm God's favor, as in the case of Joshua; they can be acts of deliverance and healing; or they can be read as acts of judgment, which is what Graham can only conclude the death of his wife must be.[19] Graham creates a false dilemma for himself: either there is ultimate meaning, and his wife has been killed as a punitive act (but in response to what?), or there is no ultimate meaning, and it's hard to say which of those options is more frightening.

Of course, we could argue (and will return to this in chapter 3, on evil) that Graham should never have taken it upon himself to assume that his family's tragedy is a sign that God is either not there or somehow vicious. Most theologians would tell you it's a dangerous thing to try to read God's will from tragic events (or perhaps from *any* events). When TV evangelist and sometime politician Pat Robertson, for example, has drawn such conclusions for God following 9/11, the Indian Ocean tsunami, and the stroke suffered by Israeli prime minister Ariel Sharon, even fellow evangelicals like Southern Baptist Convention leader Richard Land have pointed out the problems of interpretation. Land pronounced that he was "both stunned and appalled" that Robertson could "claim to know the mind of God concerning whether particular tragic events . . . were the judgments of God."[20]

But even if we don't automatically assume God's hand at work in every judgment, we also understand perfectly that a person's faith could be shaken by a tragedy—especially if that person believed that he was serving God and doing God's will. Since Graham was a priest, that means his whole identity has been shaken; for Father Graham Hess, to lose his faith is to give up who he *is*.

The movie begins with a close-up of a family picture, Graham in his clerical collar, his wife, and their two children. In an early scene, we can see the wall of Graham's bedroom, where he has taken down the cross that used to hang there—and where there is still a ghostly presence, as the paint has faded behind it. Faith may be gone, but it is not forgotten, and this film is full of such filmy reminders below the surface or at the edge of our perception. Uncertainty is often a necessary stage on the way to true faith.

When at the beginning of the movie the Hess family discovers a crop circle pressed into their cornfield, son Morgan (Rory Culkin) sets the stage for us: "I think God did it." "I think God did it," is a particularly valuable clue in *Signs*, because writer/director M. Night Shyamalan is like Alfred Hitchcock in more than just the meticulous construction of his films; he also appears in them. In *Signs*, he actually plays the essential role of Ray Reddy, who accidentally kills Graham's wife. This is the event that prompts Graham's loss of faith and the movie's plot, and it's a prime example of the clock winder showing his face.

Throughout the rest of the movie, we continue to be confronted with the question of God's existence. The film features long-held shots of the heavens as well as extreme high angle shots looking down (often called a "God's eye" view), such as the one that follows the Hess minivan into town, ending when the minivan pulls even with the church. Graham is constantly reminding people that he's "not a reverend any more," although they all want to treat him like one. During a long discussion of the alien invasion with his brother Merrill (Joaquin Phoenix), Graham reveals that he no longer believes that anyone is out there watching over them. He even says at the movie's heartbreaking Last Supper that he doesn't intend to waste another minute praying to that God who isn't there. But when Morgan has an asthma attack while the family hides from the aliens in the basement of their farmhouse, he calls out to someone: "Don't do this to me again. Not again. I hate you."

Graham has been telling everyone that he no longer believes in God, but when he's placed in this position of need, his words acknowledge something different. You don't curse someone if you don't believe that they can hear you. "That's his first step toward faith," Shyamalan notes of the scene, and Graham's dialogue during Morgan's asthma attack is both calming and incantory: Breathe. Believe. This will all be over soon. They are words that are directed to Morgan, but perhaps Graham begins to take them to heart as well.[21]

Even Morgan's asthma is part of a pattern of imagery that draws our attention to the divine. From the beginning of the film, the movie plays on traditional religious associations of wind, breath, and spirit. In Hebrew (*ruach*), Greek (*pneuma*), and Latin (*spiritus*) alike, the same word may take all three meanings; the spirit of God moving over the waters in Genesis 1:2 is sometimes also rendered breath or wind, since they are all the same word. Morgan's asthma and his ability—or inability—to breathe is a vital plot element in the movie, but wind and spirit are also evident. Through out the film, we see the corn, the trees, and the clouds moving with the wind, and the sound design (always an essential part of a Shyamalan movie) emphasizes the sound of invisible rushing air, particularly at the end of the movie.

The movie also draws our attention to water, another ancient metaphor for the sacred. Graham's daughter, Bo (Abigail Breslin), has what we might call a little obsession with fresh water that causes her to leave half-filled glasses of water all over the house— wastewater that ultimately proves to be essential in saving the family at the end of the film. In Jewish and Christian belief, water was used for ritual cleansing, and to symbolize our being brought back into communion with God. Since all three great religions of the book grew up in desert places, water is a sacred symbol in all of them. As Bruce Feiler notes in *Walking the Bible*, "Go wandering in the desert, for days, weeks, or forty years at a time and water becomes the most important thing, the only thing. Water becomes life. Becomes salvation."[22]

From "I think God did it" to the end of the film, Shyamalan is slowly and inexorably building a luminous world from details that fit together, some of them sacred symbols. It is a world in which, as Graham says, "there are no coincidences." In such a world, every element—the town veterinarian accidentally killing the wife of the priest whose son has asthma and whose daughter leaves water everywhere and whose brother was a minor league baseball slugger and whose house is invaded by an alien who secretes lethal poison gas but can't stand water—everything ultimately fits together. As in all three of Shyamalan's films of this period (the others being *The Sixth Sense* and *Unbreakable*), there is a moment of recap and epiphany in which suddenly all the unaccountable details make sense. As his dying wife had directed him, Graham finally *sees*, and what he sees is that nothing has been accidental. "That's why he had asthma," Graham is saying as he carries Morgan, whose closed lungs have repelled the alien's toxic gas, into the yard to give him an adrenaline shot, and it's why his daughter never finished a glass of water. And so on, and so on.

The final moments of *Signs* are a miracle of cinematic prowess— as we too see how all these diverse elements fit together, the simple motif that composer James Newton Howard has used throughout the movie suddenly swells, and then Shyamalan uses a grab bag of cinematic tools to allow us to know "what it feels like to feel [Graham's] epiphany."[23] Instead of the elegant tracking shots and long takes that have characterized much of the film,

Shyamalan switches to the jerky vision of a hand-held camera, and when Morgan asks, "Did someone save me?" a slight slow-motion effect drags out the moment.

"Yes," the sobbing Father Graham answers him. "I think someone did." And as Morgan's breath returns, the camera and sound track reveal the wind filling the corn, the trees, fluttering the curtain—a world full of Spirit. Then, in one seamless circular pan around the bedroom where the film began, we see the seasons change from summer to winter, and Graham steps out of the bathroom. The wall that once held the missing cross is now covered by pictures of Graham's children. He stands for a moment buttoning his black shirt, and as the shot continues and we hear the happy noises of children playing off-camera, our anticipation—our hope—builds. Then Graham turns toward us, again wearing his clerical collar, and shrugs his jacket on as he steps past us, out into the world to do God's work.

Graham needed a sign, but he needed more than that. Even a miracle isn't enough. It's what comes after the miracle. The children of Israel, marching out of Egypt and into the desert, got sign after sign, and still they griped; Jesus fed the hungry and healed the sick until he was blue in the face, and still there were doubters. So it's not simply a miracle that Graham needs; it's faith. In the faith of his family, and in the belief that grows out of the events of the film, Graham comes again to have faith that there is a God, and to recognize that if this is true, we must believe in the dark times as well as in the times when there is evidence as far as the eye can see.

Chapter Two

The Trinity
If God Exists, What Kind of God *Is* God?

Who Is This God?

In Orson Welles's *Citizen Kane* there's a moment when the entire concern of the film bubbles up to the surface for just a moment. The movie, which is told in a series of flashbacks colored by the memories of those remembering media magnate Charles Foster Kane (Welles), is an attempt at understanding a larger-than-life figure, from its opening newsreel. Was Kane a communist or a fascist? A villain or a victim? Was he a man of the people or a demagogue? A loving husband or an adulterous rogue? Kane's own take? "I am now, what I have always been—and always will be: an American."

How could a single person seem to be so many different people? In the midst of a celebratory dinner for Kane, a group of chorus girls begin singing a vaudeville tune that encapsulates that theme. "Who is this man?" the song repeats, and the answer, in the refrain, doesn't completely satisfy our curiosity any more than the movie does, but it is, at least, an answer: It's Charles Foster Kane.

In chapter 1, we examined the ways that films can show us powerful examples of a belief in the existence of a creator God. In this chapter, we'll take that idea further: If there is a God, how do we experience this God? To adapt *Kane*'s vaudeville song, Who is this God? We can come to a sort of answer like the one in *Citizen Kane*: It's God, the great "I Am." But in some ways that answer is no more satisfying than the one in the movie, and since understanding the nature of God is ultimately more important than understanding the nature of Charles Foster Kane, we're going to hope to answer it in a more useful fashion.

We've talked about God up until now in sort of an amorphous way: God is all-powerful, created the universe, cares for us. But certainly our conception of God is more complex than that, and contains contradictions we've already started to notice. Even before Jesus came on the scene, the Jews had plenty of contradictions to wrestle with. Is God the God of battles who leads the children of Israel to slaughter the inhabitants of Canaan in the book of Joshua, or the God of mercy who welcomes the repentance of the Israelites over and over again? Is God the God who spoke to Abraham, Moses, and Joshua to guide and comfort them, or the God who looks on silently as people suffer, as in many of the psalms? Although the Bible is made up of different books written at different times for different audiences, these different images of God can confound people who want to seize on a single identity.

One of the conclusions that theologians sometimes draw is that the multitude of divine images and names we come up with, even though they may seem to stand in contradiction to each other, are the best way for us to try to understand a divinity beyond our power to completely name. Nicholas of Cusa wrote that unlike human nature, which is simple and singular, God's complexity enfolds contraries. Perhaps only Charles Foster Kane knew what he truly was, how all the persons others had observed made up his unity—if in fact, he ever understood—but if God is all, then for God to be anything is to be everything, and while this may hurt our heads a little, that's the way it has to be, since ultimately "God is known to God alone."[1]

As they grappled with the identity of Jesus Christ, early Christians also had to further expand the way they thought about, prayed to, and worshiped God. If Jesus was indeed more than a righteous martyr but actually, in some sense, God, how was he God? It was a matter of constant—and continuing—discussion. Roger Olson and Christopher Hall point out how the church recognized early on a dilemma that will now look familiar: "the God whom it encountered in Jesus Christ [w]as mysterious and complex in a manner that defied human comprehension and linguistic analysis," but at least they were able to ultimately reach a critical consensus, which was that "God must exist as both a unity and a trinity."[2] In most formulations of the early church, that triune reality was described in terms of relation and action: God as Father, Son, and Spirit (or Idea, Word, Spirit). The relation between the persons, the love that binds them, we call eminent trinity, but our experience of those persons, what is revealed to us, we call economic trinity.

How can God be simultaneously a single entity and act as three? Which one of these three is Jesus? Well, the movies can actually lead us to a better understanding of the concept of the Trinity, something that more than one Christian has lost some sleep trying to grasp. We'll examine films like *The Matrix* that help us see how the Trinity might work relationally and we'll look at each distinct "person" of God through examples in movies like *To Kill a Mockingbird*, *Cool Hand Luke*, *E.T.*, and *The Fellowship of the Ring*. The attempt to understand the Trinity has involved complicated and long-lasting arguments (and much of the writing on it over the centuries should probably contain graphs and tables), but being able to see things acted out dramatically will help us a lot.

Let's begin by looking at film itself as a sort of trinitarian phenomenon. (And if you haven't yet figured this out, this would be a good place to note that the work we're doing in this book is symbolic, not allegorical; that is, the movies and things in the movies may symbolize or shed light on elements of faith, but they are not identical with them, and while we may say that a character can illustrate an aspect of God, she or he is not God but a character in a movie.) If you've ever seen a roll—or reel—of film, then you know it has a being, an ontological oneness, we might say, which is as a roll of celluloid made up of thousands of individual frames or pictures. We can look at one of these frames individually—I have a complete preview roll of the trailer to Ron Howard's *Far and Away* in my office at Baylor, and if you had the inclination, you could unroll it slowly and look at one frame and then another: There's Tom Cruise. Hey, there he is again.

But you can't see all the different frames at once—there's too much information. We don't have the capabilities, and our senses couldn't perceive them simultaneously in that way, even if we had long enough arms. It's very much like what Anselm notes in his *Proslogium* when he writes of God, "Many are these attributes: My straitened view cannot see so many at one view, that it may be gladdened by all at once."[3]

So neither can we see all the individual parts of a roll of film until they are brought to life—projected on a movie screen, incarnated into our world. When this happens, when they become linear images and sound on a screen that approximate our linear lives, we can begin to apprehend the many parts of the film stock as a unified whole: a story that (presumably) makes sense. This is how Christians think of the man called Jesus, as we shall see, as an incarnation of God into human form whose tangible life and works allow us to understand God's priorities and love for us. Through the linear life of Jesus we can begin to understand the story of God in human terms.

So we have the film stock, which is largely a mystery to us, until revealed in light and story. But what happens when we watch the projected images? Something mysterious and invisible and yet tremendously powerful. The film stock is projected as images and sound we can perceive, and we have a reaction of some sort to that confluence, an emotional, intellectual, or possibly even spiritual response. The Nicene Creed, one of the formative creeds of the early church that Christians still recite today, says that the Spirit proceeds from the Father and the Son. We might imagine the emotional reaction—laughter, tears, hope—that proceeds from those projected images as a sort of model of the Holy Spirit's action in our lives. God blows, and the Spirit enters into us to shape and move us as the wind invisibly yet powerfully flows through us. It can comfort us, challenge us, and even move us to make a difference in the world.

In all of this, the film never changes in its essential being—it's still a number of images bound in the form of a lengthy strip of cellulose—and yet it changes in how we perceive it and how it acts in us. One essential being, yet three different ways we experience it.

That's one way to begin thinking about the Trinity.

To start this cinematic discussion of who God is and how we

experience God, let's briefly consider how *The Matrix* helps us understand the workings of the Trinity. Now, clearly we can't simultaneously have three characters who are one character. But we can have three characters who possess an essential unity. In Morpheus (Laurence Fishburne), Neo (Keanu Reeves), and Trinity (Carrie-Ann Moss), we have three individuals who operate as a team, a unit, who simultaneously illustrate the movement from idea to action. According to Kathryn Tanner, the function of the Word and the Spirit is to advance the Father's idea in the world. She writes that this is how the world is "created, saved, and brought to its end or consummation": "From the Father, through the Son, in the Spirit."[4] In the *Matrix* trilogy, Morpheus is the international freedom fighter who is the father of the idea that underlies the films: that human beings should be free of the Matrix. Neo is the Son, whose wonder-working power brings that kingdom near and who ultimately sacrifices his life in *The Matrix: Revolutions* so that humans might realize that idea. Trinity is the Holy Spirit whose breath resurrects Neo when he is killed at the end of the first film, whose creative and nurturing qualities empower Neo. Together they do more than any single one could do separately, all in service of an intrinsic greater good, a universe that is just and merciful.

Still, even with illustrations the Trinity is a famously complicated and baffling concept that ultimately has to be taken on faith, whatever intellectual proofs we might offer; this is what gets Father Horvak (Brian O'Byrne) so frustrated with Clint Eastwood's questioning parishioner Frankie in *Million Dollar Baby*. Still, since the Trinity is an essential part of Christian belief, and since movies offer us plenty of these examples of relationships and characters that can enlighten us, we're going to give the intellect its shot, beginning with God the Father.

Defining God the Father

The Nicene Creed begins its discussion of the triune God in this way: "I believe in God, the Father almighty, maker of heaven and earth, of all that is, seen and unseen." Many of the ways the

Hebrews and then members of the early Christian church thought of God were derived from their being part of a patriarchal society. It meant that they couldn't conceive of an all-powerful God without imagining God as something like the most powerful people in their midst, rulers of nations or patriarchs of families. God as powerful father is not the only way we can or should think about God (God as nurturing mother is an important corrective image), and certainly for people who have had painful, abusive, or nonexistent relationships with their fathers or grandfathers it can be an actual impediment to connection with God. But it is also, as we will see, a powerful way we can imagine the divine, even if some of us may need the movies to help us connect to a powerful yet loving father figure.

The American Film Institute recently named the one hundred most important heroes and villains in movie history, and while we'll come back to villains later in the book, the number one hero in American film was the prototypical father figure, Atticus Finch (Gregory Peck) in *To Kill a Mockingbird*. When Gregory Peck passed away in 2003, many people mourned him as the father they'd never had. When we look at *To Kill a Mockingbird*, we discover that Atticus Finch exhibits several of the elements that might help us to imagine a healthy identity of God the Father—power, justice, mercy, and love.

The movie, like its source, Harper Lee's Pulitzer Prize–winning novel, is told from the point of view of Scout Finch (Mary Badham), the young daughter of Atticus Finch, and the subject matter introduced into the film early is fatherhood. What kind of father is Atticus? Well, according to his son Jem (Phillip Alford), he's too old to do anything. Not playful, nor particularly warm. Distant, even. (In the novel, Harper Lee wrote that Atticus had only one gesture of affection, ruffling Jem's hair, a gesture that is doled out very sparingly during the course of the story.) Still, as Atticus says at the beginning of the film, "I'm the only father you've got." In the course of the movie, the children learn more about Atticus as father—maybe he isn't a personal playmate, but he is a person of surprising power, absolute faithfulness, and perhaps most importantly, a paragon of justice and mercy.

Atticus's power comes as a surprise to his children. When Atticus is asked to shoot a rabid dog coming down the main street of the town, he raises the gun, sights, and shoots, and with one shot, drops the dog in its tracks. "Sure Shot Finch" Atticus used to be called, for his ability to bring the thunder of the gods. Some men with access to this kind of power would use it, often and indiscriminately. But he urges his children to be respectful of life, and the title comes from his request that they never shoot a mockingbird, since they only bring pleasure into our lives.

Atticus is identified throughout the movie as an attorney. In an early scene, an impoverished client is seen bringing him pecans as payment, and he is often seen in court, visiting clients and the families of clients, and otherwise in the pursuit of his duties. This role as attorney reminds us that one of the things that Atticus represents is inflexible justice. When called upon to defend Tom Robinson (Brock Peters), a black man, from the charge of assaulting and raping a white woman, Atticus pursues a uniform standard of justice despite the town's prejudice. Tom is not black or white in Atticus's mind; he is guilty or innocent. And if innocent—which he is—he is to be defended even at the cost of Atticus's own pain and suffering. "If I didn't," he says, "I couldn't hold my head up." Miss Maudie (Rosemary Murphy) tells the children that Atticus can always be counted on to do the right thing, even if that thing is difficult, and his defense of Tom Robinson is an example of constancy and justice.

But Atticus is not single-minded in his pursuit of justice. While he pursues what is right, he does not pursue it without considering mercy. In the Jewish rabbinic tradition, God was represented as being equally just and merciful: although "His judgments are always just," they are tempered always with mercy, and one rabbi envisioned God acting in this way: "During three hours of each day He sits and judges the whole world. When He sees that the world is deserving of being destroyed because of the prevalent evil, He arises from the throne of justice and sits on the throne of mercy."[5] In fact, there is a tradition that when the shofar—the ram's horn used in Jewish ritual—is blown, it signals God's rising from one throne and moving to the other.

Although Atticus's pursuit of justice for Tom cannot be turned aside, it too is tempered by mercy, most strikingly when he is called upon to cross-examine the accuser and supposed victim, Miss Mayella Ewell (Collin Wilcox). This poor and abused girl has suffered a horrible life, and Atticus treats her with gentleness and regards her with pity—without ever forgetting that her false accusation is putting a man's life at stake. He has the power to utterly destroy her—but that would be neither just nor merciful. Instead, he exposes the holes in her story and leaves her to her own conscience.

The movie has asked what kind of father Atticus is, and answered it: Atticus is not a playmate, nor is he warm and cuddly. But he is a father who protects his children, who stands for truth and justice, and who exhibits mercy. In the film's final scene, Atticus holds Scout on his lap, protected from all harm, a beautiful image of how God the Father might throw his arms around us as, in the Bible, God is depicted as a hen throwing her wings around her brood of chicks.[6]

The Hebrew God of battles is an aspect of God that we can imagine from many film characters, from the unstoppable warriors played by Arnold Schwarzenegger to George C. Scott's Patton, but this is a vision of God that many people of faith today have a hard time accepting. The God we see described as a fighting advocate for a particular people in Exodus, Joshua, and Judges doesn't fit well with a Christian belief that war should be a last response, and that Jesus calls us to be peacemakers, turning the other cheek and walking the extra mile.

Still, such a vision of God remains current for many people, so it's important that we discuss these images, just as we continue to read and talk about Joshua and Judges despite the violence and horror they contain. Perhaps by, again, tempering the power with mercy, we can even incorporate this vision of God the Father into our own faith. An exemplar for this might be the character of Gandalf (Ian McKellen) in *The Fellowship of the Ring*. He is a father of sorts to the other characters, wise and seemingly all-knowing, but also a figure of incredible might like the God of battles who led Israel on to victory. This power, though, is tempered by mercy.

In the Mines of Moria, Gandalf tells Frodo (Elijah Wood) that when his uncle Bilbo (Ian Holm) chose out of pity not to kill Gollum (Andy Serkis), who certainly deserved such justice, it may have been a decision that shaped the world. "Many that live deserve death, and some that die deserve life. Can you give it to them? Do not be too eager to deal out death and judgment. . . . The pity of Bilbo may rule the fate of many," he says, and in the third film of the Rings trilogy, *The Return of the King*, Gollum's continued presence is the only thing that ultimately makes it possible for Frodo to complete his quest, which is to bring in a new age of justice and possibility, free from Sauron's overarching evil. Thomas Aquinas wrote that justice and mercy always coexist in the mind of God, since "mercy does not destroy justice, but in a sense is the fullness thereof."[7] Atticus Finch and Gandalf offer us cinematic visions of how that commingling of divine mercy and judgment might operate in the being of God the Father.

The Sonship of God

You don't have to know much history to realize that the person of the Trinity that occasioned the most discussion for early Christians was God the Son. We've been talking about the Nicene Creed, but look at any of the early Christian creeds and it's easy to see where the confusion was: the person of Christ (what theologians call Christology). The 21 words we've already read from 'the Nicene Creed are the sum total of direct doctrinal teaching on God the Father. The Holy Spirit only gets 20 words. The Creed spends 133 words on Jesus, the Son of God, and people are still confused. If you know some church history, then you know that people have been involved in theological arm wrestling for two thousand years on just who—or what—Jesus was—and is, and they still are today.

When my rector, Greg Rickel, was teaching my confirmation class at St. James Episcopal in Austin, Texas, he told us that the question "Who is Jesus to me?" is the most important question a Christian can ask. So it's only appropriate, perhaps, that we have trouble settling on just what Jesus might be in relation to our understanding of God. A Christian reading of Isaiah 9 (you may know this passage from Handel's *Messiah,* if from nowhere else) usually sees the prophet's words "Wonderful Counselor, Mighty God, Everlasting Father, Prince of Peace" as references to the coming Jesus: great names, all of them, but in some tension with each other. The four canonical Gospels, Matthew, Mark, Luke, and John, present visions of Jesus that are sometimes in stark contrast to each other: the wonder-working martyr portrayed in Mark, for example, seems markedly different from the man who came from heaven portrayed in the Gospel of John. There are also noncanonical gospels relating stories of and about Jesus, such as the Gospel of Thomas and the newly restored Gospel of Judas, which expand our store of Jesuses even further, although the four Gospels chosen by the early church as authoritative offer us plenty of scope for discussion.

So as we did with the creator God, let's see if we can find some acceptable ground for seeking out images of God the Son or Jesus the Christ in film. The creedal statements tell us, first, that we are talking about someone who was at once fully God and fully man. Athanasius, in a response to Arius (an Alexandrian priest who taught, among other things, that Jesus was a human just like us who was elevated to godhood through his obedience to God), wrote that in Jesus we find "humanity and deity both at work in an incomprehensible union."[8] So we'll set our sights on images of a human being whose character might be defined by "sonship" and sacrifice and look at cinematic characters who exemplify the teaching of wisdom or performance of works of power. We'll see how in these characters that we often identify as "Christ figures," we find not just surface characteristics of Jesus but often a use of the larger message as well: that the life of this person leads to the transformation of the lives of others. Hollywood has given us many films that reflect the two primary understandings of Jesus' life and death, that of atonement and of faithful example.

In the trailer for the movie *Superman Returns,* Jor-El (the late Marlon Brando) speaks (in voice-over) in his best God the Father voice to his son, Kal-El (Brandon Routh; we know Kal-El better as "Superman"): "Even though you have been raised as a human being, you are not one of them." As coronation horns and gradually a stately pipe organ build on the sound track behind images of Superman performing marvels of strength and flight, Jor-El continues: "They can be a great people, Kal-El. They wish to be." When Superman flies upward into the sky with the blinding sun suddenly directly behind him, a moment of transfiguration such as Matthew describes when Jesus "was transfigured before them, and his face shone like the sun, and his clothes became dazzling white," Jor-El says, "They only lack the light to show the way. For this reason above all—their capacity for good—I have sent them you: my only son."[9]

If it sounds like the voice of God giving Jesus some instructions, well, it's supposed to.

The character of Superman was created by two Jewish teenagers, Jerry Siegel and Joe Shuster, in 1938, and pretty clearly the Superman character was a case of religious belief making its way into popular culture from the very beginning. I've suggested in the book *Holy Superheroes!* that Superman's life and history reflect a number of Jewish elements including the story of messiah, and David Bruce has argued that the original *Superman* (1978) "essentially retells the life of Jesus Christ."[10] The wise and beneficent Father sending his Son to earth to bring justice is already freighted with Jewish beliefs about the coming messiah and Christian beliefs about Jesus the Christ. But when you add in the use of Hebrew names for this father and son, it becomes that much more obvious. "El" is one of the names for God used in the Hebrew Bible (think about the biblical name we hear in Christmas carols, "Emmanu-El," which means "God with us"). Making "El" a sort of surname for father and son only reinforces the links. "Jor-El" might translate as either "Fear of God" or "God teaches," and "Kal-El" is very definitely a messiah's name, since it translates to "all that God is." In this trailer from *Superman Returns*, the filmmakers were very clearly tapping into this powerful religious narrative: God the Father sends God the Son to minister to human beings, to be the light in the darkness that helps them reach their full potential for good.

It's the story of Superman, but it's also the story of the gospel.

Superman, like the wonder-working Jesus of the first half of the

Gospel of Mark, is clearly a man with inhuman power to save others, but it's also power to transform through his example of service and sacrifice: "The exploits of Superman (like the lesson of Jesus) shouldn't simply evoke a passive, Gee Whiz! sort of response. They should be a call to better ourselves, and to save others, to set them free in their bodies, minds, and souls."[11] Like Jesus, Superman came to be a light to show the way and to inspire transformation.

We can see this inspiration and power to transform others in another clear "Christ figure" from contemporary Hollywood, Aslan (Liam Neeson), in *The Lion, the Witch, and the Wardrobe.* As with Kal-El, generations familiar with the story have known that one allegorical interpretation of this character is as an analogue for Jesus. Aslan is "the king of the whole wood! The top geezer! The real king of Narnia!" He's powerful and more than a little bit frightening. When toward the end of the film Mr. Tumnus (James McAvoy) says of Aslan, "He isn't a tame lion," you can feel some new understandings of what Christ—and God—might be like clicking into place.

But this powerful figure is also mortal, as we are, and his decision to sacrifice himself, a very real death at the hands of the White Witch (Tilda Swinton) to redeem the traitorious Edmund (Skandar Keynes) from her hands is the very stuff of the passion of Christ. He is ritually killed upon the great Stone Table, but the next morning he returns to life, because "when a willing victim who had committed no treachery dies in a traitor's stead, the Stone Table would crack and even Death itself would work backwards." And here of course, is the very stuff of the resurrection and its work in the world; as Paul notes in Romans 6, Christ's death and resurrection redeems us from both sin and death, and as with Superman, Aslan's life and example inspire faith and courage, particularly in the movie's battle scenes.

It's rare though that we find such full-blown expositions of theology or Christology in motion pictures; typically what we find is a character or situation that can enlighten us on one, or several, aspects of the second person of the Trinity, and that dramatic understanding is valuable for us as well. My friend Derek's favorite movie with Christian symbolism is *Cool Hand Luke*, and it does have a full slate of references to and images of Jesus. Like other movies from the 1960s and 1970s (*One Flew over the Cuckoo's Nest* is another potent example), *Cool Hand Luke* portrays a countercultural savior who performs signs and wonders, offers wisdom teaching, and transforms the lives of his followers. The movie also contains a pattern of religious imagery and reference that helps us to understand Jesus in useful ways.

Our first view of Luke (Paul Newman) comes as he drunkenly cuts the heads off a small town's downtown parking meters with a pipe cutter (like Jesus the carpenter, it looks like Luke too has specialized tools; Luke also has a bottle opener on hand to open his beer). Now clearly the Jesus we meet in the Gospels wouldn't cause a commotion like this—or would he? The Gospel of John's version of the cleansing of the Temple, a story repeated in all four Gospels, reads like this:

> In the temple he found people selling cattle, sheep, and doves, and the money changers seated at their tables. Making a whip of cords, he drove all of them out of the temple, both the sheep and the cattle. He also poured out the coins of the money changers and overturned their tables. He told those who were selling the doves, "Take these things out of here! Stop making my Father's house a marketplace!"[12]

Luke's vandalism of the parking meters comes in a similar context—parking meters often provoked controversy in small towns because they commercialized something intended to be open and public. The fact that the vendors in the Temple were performing a necessary service and that parking meters too might be a convenience doesn't change the fact that both Luke and Jesus are committing powerfully symbolic acts of rebellion—or that both of these acts ultimately lead to their deaths.

Luke is sentenced to imprisonment at the work farm, slaving away on the roads under the hot sun. Here he begins his ministry, if one can call it that. He performs a series of signs and wonders: in the "Passion of Luke," he's beaten unmercifully by Dragline (George Kennedy), the burly boss among the inmates before Luke arrives, and he achieves victory only through his willingness to suffer. Later he wins a substantial poker pot with a hand full of nothing ("Sometimes nothing can be a real cool hand," he says, prompting his new name), and in the "Miracle of the 50 Eggs," he manages to eat hard-boiled eggs (one for each prisoner) until he's near to bursting. It's an arduous task (Drag urges him at one point, "Just nine more between you and everlasting glory!"), and when he finishes he is left lying on the kitchen table, stretched out in the shape of the crucified. In other wonders, he manages to get the crew to tar a road double-time, and they find themselves having achieved symbolic freedom from captors who have no more work to impose on them as they are given leisure time for the first time in recent memory. And in the course of the film, Luke escapes three times, once remaining gone long enough to send the men a photo of himself with two beautiful women, which brings them hope and becomes a sort of sacred relic among them. Through these actions, Luke changes his fellow prisoners. He gives them an image of a better life after the life they're living, and even when he reaches the point of despair, of giving up, the other prisoners believe it's only to fool the guards.

After his capture and return, Luke and the big boss (Boss Paul, played by Luke Askew) act out a scene very much like the trial of Jesus. Boss Paul utters the famous catchphrase "What we've got here is a failure to communicate," and losing control of himself, he beats Luke. In the Gospel of John, the Roman governor Pilate finds himself unable to communicate with Jesus, and at last discovers that although he is the one who bears the world's authority, he himself is the one put on trial:

"Pilate therefore said to him, 'Do you refuse to speak to me? Do you not know that I have power to release you, and power to crucify you?'

"Jesus answered him, 'You would have no power over me unless it had been given you from above.' "[13]

Like Jesus, Luke doesn't act as though his life is in the hands of the authorities, and Boss Paul's loss of control is an indictment of his moral authority. It is indeed a failure to communicate: Boss Paul assumes that they share the same values, when clearly they don't. The prison administrators' only response to Luke's attempts to escape is to try to impose additional "rules and regulations" on him, and ultimately he would rather die than submit.

Like the image of the crucified Luke after the miracle of the eggs, other potent religious symbols appear during the course of the story. When Luke is thrown into the box for solitary confinement, he dons a nightshirt like a burial shroud and later emerges from the box into the sunlight like a man rising from the grave. Later, when forced to dig and fill a trench—his own grave, so to speak—an inmate plays the spiritual "No Grave Gonna Keep My Body Down."

When Luke escapes one last time, he takes refuge in a church, where he has a conversation with God that echoes the conversation that Jesus has with God in the Garden of Gethsemane. In the Gospel of Luke, that talk is related in this way:

"Then he withdrew from them about a stone's throw, knelt down, and prayed, 'Father, if you are willing, remove this cup from me; yet, not my will but yours be done.' "[14]

Luke's prayer to the Father is so similar that we have to assume an intentional parallel:

"Hey Old Man. . . . You made me like I am. Where am I supposed to fit in?

"On my knees, asking.

"Yeah, that's what I thought."

And when Drag, who has submitted to the authority of the bosses, enters the church and discovers his hiding place, Luke asks God, "That your answer, Old Man?"

Luke is shot and put into a car bleeding badly, yet when we see him last he has a smile on his face although he is dying. During the fight he has knocked off the mirrored sunglasses of Boss Godfrey (Morgan Woodward), the Walking Boss, who has been the everyday authority over the men on their work details. Luke has been wounded unto death, shot down like a dog, but in his shameful death, he has achieved a sort of victory over blind justice. In shattering the mirrored sunglasses that represented the implacable and unbreakable power of the law, he has freed himself and those who later follow him, as we discover. It is a victory that leads to immortality and to a cult of believers who tell and retell his story, the good news of this unlikely savior. His death does not release the men from a physical prison (any more than Jesus' death released us from the bondage and suffering of earthly life), but it does redeem them from their spiritual bonds.

In the final scene of the film, Drag shows that he resembles Peter in more than just denying his Lord in his darkest hour—he is also the apostle who answers the request for eyewitness testimony about Luke, telling the men that he was "a natural-born world shaker." The camera rises toward the heavens, and our last vision is that sacred picture of the escaped Luke, which has been folded and unfolded so often that now a cross is superimposed across his image.

It's true that wealthy and class-conscious Americans may find the figure of a criminal as savior alarming, or somehow sacrilegious, yet Jesus too was a countercultural figure. A peasant from the backcountry of Judea, Galilee, Jesus would have been a lot more like Luke or *One Flew*'s McMurphy (Jack Nicholson) than a well-groomed and well-fed politician, CEO, or even than some contemporary pastors. Although Jesus was a devoutly observant Jew, his teaching often stood in direct contrast to the established Temple cult and the Roman occupation government. Cool Hand Luke and McMurphy are not physically threatening to their societies because of their actions, any more than Jesus was to his; the crucifixion was, in some ways, a punishment out of all proportion (just as are the punishments meted out to Luke and McMurphy). But in a system that depended on order, rebellion—especially principled rebellion—could not go unpunished. A final way that Luke could stand in for Jesus is that he breaks the law (or the rules that Luke can't abide). Jesus was innocent of attempting to forcibly overthrow an existing system. But he was not innocent of standing in firm opposition to it.

Another cinematic character who dramatically illustrates many of the attributes of God the Son is E.T., the goggle-eyed alien from Steven Spielberg's blockbuster film. Like the Jesus depicted in the Gospel of John, E.T. is the man who came from heaven, an alien who can sometimes pass for one of us (throw a sheet over him, and he can go trick-or-treating) but who doesn't belong here and who ultimately must return to heaven.

.E.T. comes into the world under startling circumstances—he comes from the sky, and is left behind when his ship departs without him. He also comes into the world hunted by the authorities, as Matthew's Gospel tells us that Herod's soldiers hunted diligently for the baby Jesus. And he comes into the lives of the fractured family who take him in as the Christmas narrative in Matthew suggests: the moon hanging over the backyard shed where he hides is like the manger underneath the star.

When E.T. meets Elliott (Henry Thomas) he takes on the nature of a human through some sort of symbiosis—a connection that accounts for some of the movie's funniest and most frightening moments, and reminds us of the nature of incarnation, that incomprehensible union written about by Athanasius. But E.T. never surrenders his otherworldly nature, and like the Jesus of the Gospel of John, that nature is displayed through a series of signs. He demonstrates the power to heal: with his glowing finger (raised in the traditional visual iconography of Christ blessing) he heals Elliott when he cuts himself and brings wilted flowers back to life just as Jesus showed power to turn back death in raising Lazarus. His otherworldly nature is most clear in E.T.'s power to levitate objects—the power to fly, if you will. The film's most iconic moment, captured in the poster for the film, is when E.T. and Elliott fly across the broad face of the moon. Fans of apocalyptic rapture theology could perhaps argue that the scene, like its later twin, shows us believers taken up in the air. I'll merely observe that ascent toward heaven is a long-standing goal of spirituality, and represents an early and incomplete movement of E.T. toward home.

Finally, E.T. makes a vital sacrifice, giving up his union with Elliott when both are dying and seemingly taking his pain and suffering upon himself: although both are deathly ill, after that sacrificial act, Elliott rapidly recovers, while E.T. becomes weaker and ultimately dies, despite the best efforts of the doctors and scientists to save him.

E.T.'s death leaves Elliott bereft, and in words that might have been spoken by Jesus' apostles after the crucifixion, he says, "You must be dead. 'Cos I don't know how to feel. . . . I'll believe in you all my life. E.T., I love you." And then Elliott closes the door of the cryogenic tomb, but to those with eyes to see (and ears to hear), it becomes clear the grave can't hold E.T., as his "heartlight" begins to glow in response to the mothership returning. (This heartlight is also iconic, reminiscent as it is of depictions of the Sacred Heart of Jesus.)

In an ironic twist, Elliott and his older brother Mike (Robert MacNaughton) steal E.T.'s "body" (just as in the Gospel of Matthew the disciples were accused of plotting to steal Jesus' body to create the hoax of his resurrection) and then, trailing a shroud, E.T. steps forth, boldly backlit in Spielbergian glory, from the tomb (or at least, from the back of a white panel van).

Just as the disciples gathered for the ascension in Acts, when Jesus was taken away into heaven, Elliott's family—and the scientist who sought E.T.—gather to see him ascend in the mothership. Elliott, like Mary Magdalene who encounters the risen Jesus in John, tries to keep the risen E.T. at hand. "Stay," Elliott pleads, just as Mary tried to hold tight to Jesus and he had to tell her, "Do not hold on to me, because I have not yet ascended to the Father."[15] "But like Jesus' final promise to his disciples in the Gospel of Matthew—"And remember, I am with you always, to the end of the age"—E.T. makes a promise that he won't forsake Elliott. With that miraculous glowing finger, he touches Elliott's head in blessing and reminds him, "I'll be right here."

Here in your memory; here in your heart.

And then E.T. boards his conveyance to heaven and is borne off, but not without leaving behind another sacred sign, a rainbow. He also leaves behind a changed world. Elliott's bickering, heartsick family, who seemed ready to fall apart at the beginning of the movie, has become a loving and committed unit. Just as with Jesus' bickering disciples, E.T. brought Elliott's family together, taught them how to love without reservation, gave them courage to resist oppression, and left them with the memory that there is more than just this earthly life—that for some, at least, home is in the heavens. Like Jesus in the Gospel of John, E.T. seems to leave a great commandment—love one another as I have loved you—that is taken seriously by those believers who remain behind.

More recently, in *Spider-Man 2*, Spider-Man (Tobey Maguire) also presents an unlikely combination of natures—normal human and super-powered hero—that evokes the story of Christ. (As we observed with *Superman Returns*, superhero stories can often provide us with a valuable avatar of Jesus. Biblical scholar Burton Mack has described how the typical hero story is not that different from the Gospel of Mark's Jesus, moving from town to town, helping and healing and doing good.)[16] Spider-Man is also a man who uses his power to save others, a sacrificial hero, and a light to show the way.

Toward the end of the film, after walking off the job for a while, Spider-Man performs a life-saving rescue of a subway train full of people by using his webbing—and his body—to slow the train. It is an example of selflessness and willingness to sacrifice his life that is reminiscent of Jesus, who said, "No one has greater love than this, to lay down one's life for one's friends."[17] Jean Grey's (Famke Janssen) decision to sacrifice herself for her friends at the end of *X-2* is another example of a superhero story that meets this definition of loving sacrifice. But *Spider-Man 2* and many other superhero stories actually go farther—here Spider-Man demonstrates his willingness to give his life not just for his friends, but even for those he doesn't personally know, just as in the Gospel of Mark's depiction of the Last Supper, Jesus tells his disciples, "This is my blood of the covenant, which is poured out for many."[18] In other words, salvation is not just for those nearby and known, but is extended to those who need it, and Spider-Man puts those words into action.

Screaming in agony, arms outstretched like the cruciform sacrifice of Jesus, Spider-Man saves those aboard the train at the apparent cost of his own life. Those inside the train pull him gently within, where he is passed from hand to hand overhead, as though taken gently down from the cross. To the accompaniment of horns and a ghostly chorus, he is laid to rest on the floor of the subway car—and then he comes back to life. Rising, he realizes that he has lost his mask, but two children bring it forward. "We won't tell nobody," one says, and the gathered crowd agrees. Then he says, "It's good to have you back, Spider-Man."

Peter Parker has again combined the supernatural power with his human nature, and has again put the safety and well-being of others—all others—ahead of his own. "With great power comes great responsibility," Peter's Uncle Ben once told him, and like Mark's Jesus, he will now again use his power to help others—even at the expense of himself.

Chasing the Spirit

These examples of cinematic analogues help us see God as creator, father, bringer of justice, bearer of mercy; they help us to understand Jesus as son, miracle worker, healer, martyr, bringer of justice, loving friend. Although we will find useful examples in the movies, Spirit is a bit more of a theological challenge. Step into any church using the Revised Common Lectionary on Trinity Sunday and watch the preacher stumble over a message on the Holy Spirit—if in fact she or he preaches on the Spirit at all. Although the Holy Spirit is still almost universally accepted as the third person of the Holy Trinity, she (for balance and out of personal preference, I'll be using feminine pronouns in this discussion of the Spirit) has always gotten short shrift compared to Father and Son. Hendrikus Berkhof wrote that this topic, "more than any other, causes a feeling of deep embarrassment in the mind of a theologian who dares to ponder it," and Rowan Williams has written with a degree of understatement that there is "a certain poverty in theological reflection on the Holy Spirit."[19] We'll again try to redress this difficulty by locating dramatic examples that can help us understand this enigmatic person of the Trinity.

The Gospel of John, the only place in the Gospels where formal instruction about the Spirit appears, identifies the Spirit by using the Greek word *paraclete* (παράκλητος), which referred in the ancient world to a defense attorney or advocate, and is often translated "comforter," although the word doesn't do justice to the full range of Greek meanings. A paraclete is a helper and a consoler, as well as an advocate. Chapter 16 of John announces that the paraclete will extend Jesus' teaching into the world and help the disciples better understand truth.[20] But many understandings of the Spirit begin and end at the point of inspiration and illumination.

Augustine, in the opening of *The Confessions*, wrote that the Spirit impels us to seek God: "You move [us] to take pleasure in praising you, because you have made us for yourself, and our hearts are restless until they rest in you."[21] One view of the role of the Spirit is indeed, as Mark Pinsky describes Jiminy Cricket in *Pinocchio*, as one's "designated conscience," a still, small voice that directs us to do what we know is right.[22] In the church of my childhood and still in some churches today, this is the primary role attached to the Spirit, that of heavenly nag and cheerleader, lifting the hearts of worshipers and prodding those who need to make a spiritual decision to step forward toward the front of the church before everybody's lunch burns.

But as Rowan Williams observes, to limit our conception of the Spirit to a belief that she merely leads us in charismatic worship, prompts understanding, or represents our conscience is to greatly impoverish our understanding of the Trinity. The Spirit, Williams says, must take on more than simply "a mediatorial or an episodically inspirational role." Ultimately, the Spirit is given us to help us become more Christian—to move our own lives in the direction of the cruciform shape of the life of Christ and to help us to emulate or conform to that life.[23] And Berkhof offers this definition of the Holy Spirit prompted by the translation of the Greek *pneuma*, that the Spirit is "God's inspiring breath by which he grants life in creation and re-creation."[24]

The Spirit, then, does encourage us in the direction of God— and also consoles, inspires, and sustains us in that quest. She *enables* (in the pre–self-help meaning of the verb) us to do Christ's work and be Christ's people in the world. And by examining a few of these enabling and inspirational characters in Hollywood films, we should gain a greater understanding of how God moves in our lives through spirit.

Two feminine archetypes come immediately to mind in this regard: mothers (who often encourage, inspire, console, and nag, all in one conversation) and muses (who inspire and aid). The sort of archetypal mother played by Donna Reed on television (or by Joan Crawford in *Mildred Pierce* or Meryl Streep in *One True Thing*), whose life, energy, and creativity revolve around her family, might offer us a vision of the nurturing and comforting Spirit who pushes us toward growth and right behavior. Although mother figures in the films of Alfred Hitchcock are often problematic characters (one thinks immediately of *Psycho*'s Mrs. Bates), Doris Day's Jo in the 1956 remake of *The Man Who Knew Too Much* exemplifies the inspiring, creative, and sustaining power of the Spirit as she teaches her child to sing, pursues him when he is lost, and finally draws him back to her by the sound of her voice (in the film's famous conclusion, as she interminably sings "Que Sera, Sera"). In Hitchcock's *Spellbound*, Dr. Constance Petersen (Ingrid Bergman) functions as a combination mother and muse to Gregory Peck's John Ballantine. Gently and lovingly she nurtures him and leads him toward healing. Lisa Carol Fremont (Grace Kelly) in *Rear Window* makes her first appearance with a kiss, then lights up the darkness of his apartment for Jeff Jeffries (Jimmy Stewart). Like the other Hitchcock women we've mentioned, she not only nurses, she also inspires and encourages Jeff, making it possible for him to pursue their common quest for justice and truth—and also, finally, to push past his unwillingness to love another unselfishly.

Not all of our cinematic images of a sustaining and inspiring Spirit have to be feminine, of course. Rafiki, in *The Lion King*, is a potent analogue for the Spirit. In the movie's opening scene, when he holds up the baby Simba, he becomes the first to recognize and draw attention to the new lord, and the visual iconography, as the sun breaks through the heavens, reminds us of the New Testament passages about Jesus' baptism, when the sky was torn apart, the Spirit descended, and the Father said, "You are my Son, the Beloved; with you I am well pleased."[25] Later in the film, after Simba has been driven away from the pridelands, Rafiki performs other traditional functions of the Spirit, showing the Son the Father and, ultimately, revealing the Son to himself.

"I know your father," Rafiki tells the grown Simba.

"My father is dead," Simba tells him, but Rafiki hoots.

"Nope! He's alive. I'll show him to you." Rafiki leads Simba to a pool of water and tells him, "Look down there."

"You see, he lives in you!" Rafiki tells him.

Then, when Simba hears the Godlike voice of his father, he sees his father's image in the heavens. The voice tells him to look inside himself and to take his rightful place in the world. "Remember who you are."

By showing the son the father, by reminding him that he is more than he seems, that he has another nature and a kingly and sacrificial destiny, Rafiki allows Simba to do the work he has been called to do from the beginning of his life on Earth.

A final cinematic version of Spirit shows up in *Schindler's List*, where Itzhak Stern (Ben Kingsley) serves as Oskar Schindler's conscience, prompting Schindler (Liam Neeson) always toward compassion and encouraging him to believe that his actions are necessary and good. It is Stern who shares with Schindler the Talmudic wisdom that, "Whoever saves one life saves the entire world," Stern who confirms that Schindler is right in what he is doing: "The list is life." (And in the sense of enabling Schindler, it is Stern's accounting skill, understanding of business, and contacts among the Polish Jews that allows Schindler to succeed in saving so many from death at the hands of the Nazis.) We've said we might understand the role of Spirit as pushing us toward a more Christlike life, encouraging us, and giving us strength to persevere; if Stern can push the bad Catholic Oskar Schindler toward a more Christlike life, then we can see the way the Spirit might also nudge and enable us toward a life worth living.

We come back, at last, to Kane. At the end of *Citizen Kane*, the reporter, Thompson (William Alland), who has spent the entire movie gathering information on the deceased tycoon, tells others that he never did find out exactly who Charles Foster Kane was. He was all the things that people said, identities held in tension, and while he had hoped the search for Kane's last word, "Rosebud," would open complete understanding for him, he has decided against it. It would have been another piece of the puzzle. And perhaps so it is for us and for the Trinity: three pieces, each substantial, each different, fitting together, together forming a complete picture.

And like Kane, God is ultimately unknowable, even if we have a library of movies to choose characters from. But the creeds of the church and our common beliefs have given us three names to praise and to meditate upon, and to imagine a father like Atticus Finch, a sacrificing savior like Superman, and a comforting inspiration like Grace Kelly's Lisa Carol Fremont is to begin, at least, to imagine the awesome power, goodness, and beauty that is God.

Chapter Three

Sin and Death
If God Is Good, Where Did Evil Come From?

Sin Enters the Garden

She slips away from the others at the beach party and down to the ocean. The moon shines on the water, lapping serene at the shore. She slips out into those waves, takes a step, then another. Then she begins to swim, slowly, gratefully, the saltwater cradling her like a mother. One moment, there's nothing but beauty. The next: horror. Something grabs her. Hard. It pulls her under. It takes a piece of her away. And the next thing she knows, it has her in its clutches, is hauling her away to her destruction.

It's a beautiful world that the great white shark enters into in Steven Spielberg's *Jaws*, an idyllic world of beaches and small towns and holidays, an Eden, we might say. But what we're talking about now is the story of sin and death, told and retold throughout the ages, and in this story, something dark and dangerous always shows up to mock the world's perfection, almost as though it had to be.

In the garden of Eden story told in the second and third chapters of the book of Genesis, two people, a man and a woman, are living in a perfect world, in close relationship with the God who created them and it. Then, tempted by the crafty serpent, the woman does what God has commanded them not to do: She eats a fruit from the tree of the knowledge of good and evil. Why does she do it? Well, the simple answer—and the simplistic one—is that the serpent tempted her, and that's the answer she gives to try to get off the hook: "The serpent tricked me, and I ate."[1] The aftermath of this sin in the Eden story is that this beautiful and perfect existence where we walked together with God is ended; pain, suffering, and death enter human experience for the first time. The perfect creation, welcoming and kind, became something ominous and dangerous to humankind. According to Hildegard of Bingen, after that, "Creation opposed Man because he rebelled against God," so that "the elements of the world which before had existed in great calm, were turned to the greatest agitation and displayed horrible terrors."[2]

And so it remains today; this fall in Eden has long-lasting consequences in both the Jewish and the Christian self-understanding. The medieval rhyme went, "Through Adam's fall/We sin-ned all"; the apostle Paul describes the equation similarly: "Sin came into the world through one man, and death came through sin, and so death spread to all because all have sinned."[3]

The depiction of evil in the movies is more than just an effective deployment of conflict, a story element that keeps audiences riveted to the action on the screen; it also can show us a theological reflection of the sin and death that theologians and people of faith talk about. Sin and death are the ultimate problems to be grappled with in thinking about a world with a beneficent God, and so we'll look at films that illustrate all the elements of sin we've mentioned, and we'll attempt to grapple with what the movies have to say about the presence of evil in the world. Through a closer look at films like *Double Indemnity*, *Psycho*, *The Godfather*, *The Silence of the Lambs*, and the *Star Wars* and *Lord of the Rings* epics, we'll investigate some of Hollywood's depictions of evil. Finally, by attention to Steven Spielberg's *Schindler's List* and *Munich*, we'll see how our most popular filmmaker's most challenging films continue to demonstrate keen insight into the ways sin enters our world—and the consequences of it.

The word "evil" appears in hundreds of Bible verses and liberally dusts the works of the Hebrew Bible, the Apocrypha, and the Christian Testament. The Hebrew word for evil typically refers to the opposite of good or righteous; the Greek words variously translated as "evil" include terms more precisely meaning harm, wickedness, and wrong. But however we think of evil—as unrighteousness, harmfulness, or wickedness—we can find examples in Hollywood film.

"Sin," also appears in hundreds of verses in the Bible. The problem of sin pervades the early sections of the Hebrew Bible and even causes God to flood the world in a vain attempt to get rid of it. He decides after the flood that he can't, that sin is embedded in human nature, and so he concedes: "I will never again curse the ground because of humankind, for the inclination of the human heart is evil from youth."[4] Other Old Testament writers agree with God's assessment. The author of Proverbs says, "Who can say, 'I have made my heart clean; I am pure from my sin?' " and the writer of Ecclesiastes concurs: "Surely there is no one on earth so righteous as to do good without ever sinning."[5] For whatever reason, Hebrew thinkers accepted that sin was a part of this created world; some early Christian thinkers, however, leaned toward a supernatural explanation, an idea that something must be working against us (and against God) to explain our bad behavior, the persecution of God's faithful, and why the world just didn't work the way it should. As E. P. Sanders notes, in the Letter to the Romans the apostle Paul seems to personify sin "as a power which is not only alien from God but which is almost as potent; in fact it often wins the struggle," and in Paul's discussion of sin and Satan, Paul demonstrates that he was at the very least influenced by dualistic ways of seeing the problem of good and evil.[6]

For many people the most compelling explanation for sin is the presence of a supernatural tempter, a powerful outside influence, something, at least, that is not us pulling the strings; like Han Solo (Harrison Ford) in *The Empire Strikes Back*, we'd love to be able to shout, "It's not my fault!"

In the Christian mythos, we call that supernatural tempter "Satan"; in the Hebrew Bible, when the character of Satan appears, it is as an adversary or accuser, which is the literal Hebrew meaning of the word. (Like "paraclete," the Greek word meaning "advocate" used to name the Holy Spirit, the Hebrew word "satan" is also a sort of legal term, very much like a prosecutor.) Joanne K. Kuemmerlin-McLean writes that the Satan character we find throughout the Hebrew Bible "serves primarily as a judicial 'adversary' acting at God's request."[7] In places in the Christian Testament, Satan seems to continue this testing function, but as Elaine Pagels has persuasively argued, the writers of the Gospels took the Jewish character and altered him to personify evil, and introduced a character into Judeo-Christian thought who stood in opposition to the good that God willed for creation.[8] Satan causes people to sin. So it is that Judas Iscariot, the betrayer of Jesus, is represented in the Gospel of John as someone Satan leads into final treachery at the Last Supper: "After he received the piece of bread, Satan entered into [Judas]. Jesus said to him, 'Do quickly what you are going to do.' "[9] And Judas went off to betray his master.

Temptation is indeed a powerful force. As I write these words, I have a powerful hankering for some greasy barbecue, and I'd like to blame the barbecue and not my feeble willpower. Augustine, in his meandering way toward truth, wrote how in his youth

> It pleased my pride to be beyond blame, and not to confess myself to have done it when I had done something morally wrong. Had I confessed it, You would have cured my soul, since it was a sinning against You. But I loved to excuse myself and to accuse something else—I know not what—that was present with me but was not what I was.[10]

Oscar Wilde is supposed to have said, "I can resist anything except temptation," and Mae West, "I generally avoid temptation unless I can't resist it." A dark supernatural power who tempts us into evil actions is a compelling solution to two of the central problems of Christian theology: If God is good, then why do pain and evil exist? And, on a more personal note, Why do I do the things I know I shouldn't?

This first question, why bad things happen under the watch of a good God, is commonly called theodicy, and it emerges not just from our understanding of God as a benevolent God, but also from our desire to perceive meaning in our existence. If things happen for a reason—any reason—then we can sleep a little more soundly. But, if, as Father Hess once imagined in *Signs*, there is no meaning to the universe, then how are we to shape our lives?

This problem of seeking meaning in the face of randomness is the problem facing the Jarrett family in *Ordinary People*, Robert Redford's Academy Award–winning directorial debut. Drawn from the powerful novel by Judith Guest, the film depicts Conrad Jarrett (Timothy Hutton), who somehow survived the boating accident that claimed the life of his brother Buck, and his parents Beth and Calvin (Mary Tyler Moore and Donald Sutherland) as they try to make sense of the unaccountable entry of death into their lives. Conrad is filled with such sadness and guilt that he has attempted suicide, his mother has withdrawn from him into the memories of her beloved older son, and the father can only stand and watch as his family begins to fall apart.

Often people's helpful responses to this grief are no help. When a friend tells Beth that everyone just wants for her to be happy, she snarls, "Happy! Ward, you tell me the meaning of happy. But first you better make sure your kids are good and safe, that they haven't fallen off a horse, been hit by a car, or drowned in that swimming pool you're so proud of!" And other "helpful" responses people sometimes make to suffering and death (especially someone else's suffering) are that these trials and heartaches are somehow "God's will," that God is testing a person or a family, or that God somehow needed Bucky in heaven. It is an affront to our puzzled humanity to begin to understand, as the psychiatrist Dr. Berger (Judd Hirsch) tells Conrad, that sometimes these things just happen.

We want evil, suffering, and death to be somebody's fault, if only to reassure ourselves that we can discern some structure to the universe we inhabit. It's why we investigate plane crashes, levee failures, acts of nature as well as acts of terrorism. We want to know why bad things happen.

There is an answer, of course—if there is evil and death in the world, perhaps we are responsible for it. But since I don't know if we're ready for that slap in the face just yet, let's get back to God and Satan for a moment.

It's a thorny theological problem if we imagine that evil and death are somehow God's intention. As preacher and activist William Sloane Coffin said in a justly famous sermon on the death of his son, this was *not* God's will, and as Augustine reminded us back in chapter 1, God made all things good.[11] How then could we associate this benevolent God with evil and death? Ah, but if we can say that there is an evil force in the universe that is not God, but that *contends* against God, that wants to undo the good in creation, then suddenly the deaths and disasters might begin to fall into place more easily, as might our inability, as the apostle Paul wrote, to do what is right, even though we know what is right.[12] It's here where "that ancient serpent, who is called the Devil and Satan, the deceiver of the whole world" comes into play for us, and it's here, with powerful supernatural evil, that we'll begin our journey.[13]

The Devil and Supernatural Evil

Satan has sometimes appeared as himself in the movies (*Rosemary's Baby*, *Devil's Advocate*), but it generally doesn't work any better than that angel thing we talked about earlier. As Walter Wink has noted, "Nothing commends Satan to the modern mind," and Satan's character is now hopelessly dopey, tangled in hooves and horns, in his use as sports mascots and as the crimson-skinned gay lover of Saddam Hussein in *South Park: Bigger, Longer, and Uncut*.[14] But we can see frightening and dramatically successful depictions of Satan without breaking out the hooves and horns. Why, what else is Keyser Soze, the supernatural bogeyman of *The Usual Suspects*? "Keyser Soze. The devil himself," one of his victims screams, and I'm not disinclined to believe him.

We can find another potent account of supernatural temptation in Peter Jackson's *Lord of the Rings* trilogy. To an even greater degree than in Tolkien's three *Rings* novels, Jackson dramatically emphasizes the motif of temptation in his films: through the One Ring, the power of the Dark Lord Sauron sends out a call to almost every major character to take the ring and use it for her or his own purposes. And if he or she does, while the immediate result of temptation might be gratification, as it often is, the ultimate result is sure to be the kind of personal decay and desolation we see demonstrated graphically in the character of Gollum (Andy Serkis).

On a recent hike in the North Carolina woods, after we had been climbing quietly for some time, my son Chandler asked, out of nowhere, "Is Gollum good or bad?" I had been thinking about the light filtering through the leaves, not *The Lord of the Rings*, and so I didn't answer him immediately. We walked on for a bit before he answered himself: "He's both."

"Okay," I said, nodding. "Sometimes he's one, and sometimes he's the other. It just depends." While Tolkien had hinted at this split in the character's personality, at times Jackson's camera angles actually split the character voiced by Andy Serkis into "Gollum" and "Smeagol," depending on whether the bad or good side of the character is talking, whether the creature is under the sway of the Ring's deadly temptation or able to see clearly and respond to kindness with kindness. From the very beginnings of his "life," when the creature Smeagol murdered his best friend Deagol for the glittering Ring, "Gollum" displays what happens when one gives in to the temptation to sin: One throws away the ability to act with justice and mercy, or to have any concern larger than oneself. Like Gollum, like the wizard Saruman (Christopher Lee), like the once-human Ringwraiths who accepted the rings of power tied to the One Ring, giving in to temptation may even lead to one's destruction. It's an old, old story.

But *The Lord of the Rings* films, although they present a powerful Dark Lord, do not postulate an all-powerful tempter. Gollum, Saruman, and others, do ultimately fall victim to temptation, but many of those enticed by the Ring in the three films display strength of character and spiritual acuity. They—as Galadriel (Cate Blanchett) says after Frodo (Elijah Wood) offers her the Ring in *The Fellowship of the Ring* and she manages to decline it—"pass the test." Still, cinematic devices like close-ups of the Ring, smash-cuts of the Eye of Mordor, and ominous camera angles dramatically reveal the inner struggles that these characters endure. Galadriel, Gandalf, and Bilbo (Ian Holm) all wrestle with the temptation of the Ring. Aragorn (Viggo Mortensen) worries that as the heir to Isuldur, the man who kept the Ring when he should have destroyed it, he is subject to the same fate, and the temptation later brings him to his knees when Frodo confronts him with that desire.

The gentle and generous Frodo's slow descent into himself in the second and third films as he carries the Ring reveals its insidious power to pull people toward the darkness.

Even characters like Frodo, good people, noble people, give in to temptation, for no one is perfect. The human warrior Boromir (Sean Bean) yields to the siren call when he tries to take the Ring from Frodo, and Boromir's brother Faramir does so in *The Two Towers* when he learns about the Ring and decides to bring Frodo and the Ring back to his land to use against the Dark Lord (an incident that does not take place in the novel, where Faramir quickly "shows his quality" just as Galadriel had earlier).[15] But one may yield to temptation and then choose to push it away. Boromir dies nobly, selflessly, in defense of others, a death that refutes the selfish temptation to which he momentarily succumbed. ("You have kept your honor," Aragorn assures him as he lies dying.) Likewise, at the conclusion of *The Two Towers*, Faramir is able to turn Frodo loose to resume his mission to Mordor, despite that long detour and the indecision that has stayed his hand. And although Aragorn has told his love Arwen (Liv Tyler) that "the same blood flows in me" as in his ancestor, she tells him—truly—that he will overcome it. Supernatural evil is strong—but some things are stronger yet.

A similar examination of the possible power of supernatural evil is shown in the Harry Potter films. In *Harry Potter and the Goblet of Fire*, Alastor Moody (Brendan Gleeson), the new Defense Against the Dark Arts teacher, demonstrates the three unforgivable curses for Harry (Daniel Radcliffe) and his class. There is the Cruciatus curse, the torture that causes excruciating pain; there is the Avracadavra curse, the killing curse that Harry magically survived as an infant. And there is the Imperius curse. "Gave the Ministry quite a bit of grief a few years ago," Moody tells his first-day students. "Perhaps this will show you why."

He casts the Imperius curse on an enlarged spider and then proceeds to put on a show with her, vaulting her around the classroom at his whim from shrieking student to shrieking student. "What shall I have her do next?" he asks at last. "Jump out the window? Drown herself?"

The class draws silent as the spider hovers above a pot of water.

And so Moody concludes his demonstration: "Scores of witches and wizards have claimed that they only did You-Know-Who's bidding under the influence of the Imperius Curse. But here's the rub: How do we sort out the liars?"

In other words: how do we reconcile people's behavior with the claim, "The devil made me do it"? Voldemort (Ralph Fiennes) and his Death Eaters could employ the Imperius curse to impose their will on other wizards—but how many wizards simply used the screen of supernatural evil as an excuse for their own choices?

At the end of *Harry Potter and the Sorcerer's Stone*, Voldemort presents Harry with perhaps his ultimate temptation. Earlier, Harry has seen his mother and father, who were killed by Voldemort when he was an infant, alive in an enchanted mirror that shows a person's deepest desires. Now Voldemort asks, "Would you like to see your mother and father again? Together we can bring them back. All I ask is for something in return."

It's a lie of course—no spell can bring the dead back to life—but Harry is an inexperienced wizard, and doesn't know that yet.

All the same, Harry refuses to give him that "something"—the Sorceror's Stone, which will bring Voldemort into a physical body after his long half-life—but the temptation must have been a potent one. How many of us would be able to resist, if offered what we most desired?

The *Star Wars* films demonstrate that power of temptation as well. The Dark Lords of the Sith do not employ Jedi mind tricks—the Imperius Curse, so to speak—to force people to do their dark bidding. In *The Empire Strikes Back*, Darth Vader (David Prowse/James Earl Jones) attempts to persuade Luke (Mark Hamill) that they should rule the galaxy together using only his words and the threat of force. In *The Revenge of the Sith*, Chancellor Palpatine (Ian McDiarmid), powerful as he may be, uses no more than tempting words and Anakin Skywalker's (Hayden Christensen) own fear of loss to turn him to the dark side.

Although elsewhere we see Jedi messing with "weak minds," these Dark Lords tempt their prey using what they know they want, sometimes even appealing to what is good. Temptation is not always toward something low, degrading, or stereotypically sinful, and this temptation toward the good—although not perhaps, the right—is what Walter Wink describes as the truly satanic. When Satan tempts Jesus in the Gospel of Matthew, he is not prompting him toward things he should not want—loose women, a gas-guzzling Hummer   but toward things that would reveal him as the sort of Messiah everyone expects him to be: "What is Satan tempting him with here and in each of these 'temptations,' " Wink writes, "if not *what everyone knew to be the will of God*?"[16]

Vader offers Luke the chance to overthrow the Emperor and rule at his father's side; Luke resists that temptation. But earlier in the saga, that father, Anakin Skywalker, was tempted by and succumbed to his desire to protect his wife Padme (Natalie Portman) from death in childbirth and became Darth Vader. Both are potent desires—the temptations are toward palpable goods. But they are both essentially selfish desires, and there are higher goods. Luke sees that, perhaps fortified by the knowledge of his father's failure, and resists; Anakin does not, and falls, ultimately causing the death that he had foreseen and feared. But each does so by his own choice.

As compelling (and exculpatory) as magical explanations might be, then, ultimately sin and evil cannot be explained by supernatural temptation; even if one believes in Satan as a powerful force of evil, one does not have to listen to him.

A simple extra-personal temptation is thus incomplete, even if one believes in the existence of Dark Lords, talking serpents, or of an adversary to God called Satan. It smacks too much of the solution imagined by the Persian Zoroastrians, Augustine's Manicheans, or the gnostics: that the universe holds two deities who are locked in immortal struggle, one of them evil, one of them good, and that we are somehow caught up in their chess match. Although evil is powerful, Augustine concluded that sin was not imposed on him from without, that evil was not extra-personal: "In truth however, I was my whole self; and it was my impiety that divided me against myself."[17] Hendrikus Berkhof argues that sin comes into being from our own personal sinfulness, through unhealthy interpersonal interactions, and for supra-personal reasons, including corrupted

institutions and cultural understandings in which we allow ourselves to be caught.[18]

Evil and the Human Experience

The Eden story thus illustrates four understandings of sin's genesis, not just the supernatural one many Christians consider to be
primary. In its tale of the serpent's temptation to evil, it does allow
for the possibility of outside, even supernatural agency; in its
description of Eve's decision to disobey (because with her own
eyes she saw that the fruit was beautiful and because she desired
the wisdom that God possessed), it tells us about personal failure;
by describing the collusion between husband and wife in his decision to take and eat and in their mutual attempt to hide this from
God, we see the interpersonal aspect of sin, as their relationship
leads them both to compound their personal sin; and one could
even argue, as some have done, that they are part of a system or
institution that encourages their moral failure (giving us a supra-
personal vision of sin.)

One of the Hollywood genres that can tell us much about sin is
film noir, shadowy films that began with John Huston's *The Maltese Falcon* and include Billy Wilder's *Double Indemnity* and *Sunset Boulevard,* Orson Welles's *Touch of Evil,* Roman Polanski's
Chinatown, and contemporary films such as *L.A. Confidential* and
Sin City. Often set in sunny Southern California, these films
employ stark visual contrasts between light and shadow to evoke
the stark contrasts between good and evil, and they evince a the-
matic understanding of the dark underbelly of American society
that often finds expression in stories of greed, adultery, violence,
and murder.

Like *The Maltese Falcon, The Big Sleep,* and *Sin City, Double
Indemnity* is a *film noir* drawn from pulp fiction, in this case the
hard-boiled novella by James M. Cain about an insurance salesman who is seduced by a client's wife—or who seduces himself—
into trying to crock the system by killing the client and collecting
on his life insurance. In *Double Indemnity,* Fred MacMurray (who
later played Disney movie heroes and the iconic dad on the TV

series *My Three Sons*) expanded his usual good-guy persona to play unscrupulous insurance man Walter Neff, and Barbara Stanwyck donned an improbable blonde wig to portray Phyllis Dietrichson, who is either a temptress (the femme fatale often found in such films) or a powerful and liberated female—or both. Separately and together, Walter and Phyllis fall into sin that dooms and damns them.

What is sin? In the Hebrew Bible, sin falls into one of two major categories: falling away from the worship of the one true God to pursue idols, or pursuing piety at the expense of justice; both seem to be about following one's own desires rather than pursuing the will of God. For Thomas Aquinas, sin was caused by "the inordinate love of self," while *The Book of Common Prayer* actually defines sin as "the seeking of our own will instead of the will of God."[19] Berkhof agrees that sin is egotism, but he broadens the scope to say that sin comes "through our egotism as individuals, groups, races, and nations."[20] Sin and evil come into the world because of the misuse of human freedom, and in *Double Indemnity*, Walter Neff becomes a big-league sinner because he makes very bad choices designed to gratify his own ego.

Our Edenic myth of sin suggests that spotless creatures were tempted, succumbed, and fell; one could perhaps read the opening scenes of *Double Indemnity* in this way. Walter Neff seems a likeable sort, funny, the kind of person you'd want to have a beer with, perhaps. He has a good friend in the office, an insurance genius played by Edward G. Robinson. Neff certainly doesn't seem like the kind of person who would kill a man for a woman and for money, as he tells his office Dictaphone at the beginning of the film. But then all of a sudden there is Phyllis, flashing her long legs at him and later cracking wise with him as though they are actually prospective lovers in a screwball comedy instead of prospective adulterers. We can even be sympathetic to these two up to a certain point: the point at which it becomes clear that they're talking about murdering Phyllis's husband to collect the double indemnity for accidental death, the kind almost no one ever manages to collect because that kind of death, as Robinson's character memorably attests, almost never happens. It's then that Walter's pride overflows; why should he break his back selling insurance to suckers when he's smart enough to outsmart the system?

Augustine is famous for having tried to squeeze the toothpaste of human pride so that it led inexorably to the evil action of lust, and we might imagine that lust is a sin being acted upon with some regularity in *Double Indemnity*. We might thus imagine that lust is the tinder that ignites all of the sins in the film, of which there are indeed many. But even allowing for the restrictions of the Production Code, which forbade filmmakers of the period from portraying extramarital sexual conduct (or much of any sexual conduct), Neff and Dietrichson seem to have little sexual interest or energy for each other even as they play lovers who are crazy for each other.[21] No, what makes the action of *Double Indemnity* particularly chilling is that this can't be mistaken for a crime of passion: Phyllis wants the money (and to be rid of Walter once she has it); Walter wants to see, after all this time on the other side of the curtain, if he is smart enough to get away with murder and crock his insurance company.

So clearly personal evil is at work here; both Walter and Phyllis are guilty of pursuing their own desires no matter where they might lead. But Berkhof's thoughts about the dynamics of sin are useful: as he notes, "we do not sin all by ourselves."[22] It is easy to put aside the "female temptress" argument—like the female leads in *The Postman Always Rings Twice*, *Body Heat*, and other *films noir*, Phyllis is a temptress who wants her man to do something bad for her, but *Double Indemnity* makes it clear that Walter *chooses* to kill Mr. Dietrichson—although it certainly seems possible to assert that each of these two is more evil when they are together than apart. Popular psychology sometimes talks about "enabling" behavior, which is a good description of the relationship between Walter and Phyllis. Apart, Walter might have dreamed of beating the system, but until he met Phyllis, he probably would not have acted upon those sinful desires. It is a fatal encounter that ultimately leads not just to the death of Phyllis's husband, but to both of their deaths. Walter shoots Phyllis shortly after she tells him she loves him, and a deleted scene featured MacMurray being led away to the gas chamber.

Although it is less noticeable, sin also emerges from a societal factor in *Double Indemnity*. While Phyllis and Walter, like Luke and Anakin, bear the ultimate responsibility for their choices, they inhabit sunny Southern California, a society that exalts sex, greed, and self-gratification as its highest values. The provocative title of Reinhold Niebuhr's *Moral Man and Immoral Society* suggests that while individuals may choose or reject individual evils, it is possible that simply belonging to a society may lead them toward evil choices. In nineteenth-century America, for example, during the times of slavery and the expansionist Mexican War, Henry David Thoreau wrote, "Law never made men a whit more just; and, by means of their respect for it, even the well-disposed are daily made agents of injustice."[23] In an immoral society, simply following the lead of others may lead one to be an agent of evil. So it was that Dietrich Bonhoeffer chose to actively resist the Nazi government of his native Germany, and Martin Luther King Jr. to argue that segregation might be the law of the land but it was an immoral law that made sinners of all who obeyed it. While we will examine other, more powerful examples of societal sin in the movies, *Double Indemnity* does reflect individuals who simply—if sinfully—take the values of their society to their ultimate end.

Walter Neff is handsome, funny, lovable, and ultimately, a damned soul. While many of the characters we'll discuss in this chapter are larger than life and scary as hell—we've already mentioned Sauron, Voldemort, Darth Vader, and Bruce the Shark, and Hannibal the Cannibal is right around the corner (we could add Cruella de Ville as well, but I think women have been villainized enough since that whole Eve story started)—one of the equally scary notions that has emerged in the aftermath of the Final Solution and the Manhattan Project is the banality of evil. It's one thing to think of Satan with his bright red union suit and flames dancing at his hooves. But the bow-tied bureaucrats who made the cattle cars run on time in Nazi Germany, the pipe-smoking nuclear physicists who played tennis at Los Alamos when they weren't building the bomb that would cremate Hiroshima? Those are people who could be just like us. Everyday. Ordinary. Normal, even.

And yet their actions led to the deaths of millions.

The phrase "the banality of evil" first entered the language as philosopher Hannah Arendt covered the trial of the Nazi Adolph Eichmann for *The New Yorker*. Eichmann was one of those responsible for sending the Jews of Germany and Occupied Europe to the death camps, but what outraged Arendt about witnessing his trial was not that the things he did were so horrifying, although they certainly were. What caught her attention was how ordinary and routine these acts seemed to him. How everyday. How bureaucratic: "He did his *duty* . . . he not only obeyed *orders*, he also obeyed the *law*."[24]

He didn't hate the Jews; he was just doing his job.

Arendt's conclusion was that many of the Nazis who did horrific things were not psychopathic, at least as we popularly understand the term. They appeared to be no different from you or me.

Average.

Normal, even.

Likewise, what makes the films of Alfred Hitchcock so frightening is not graphic violence. Although today we flash immediately to the shower scene in *Psycho* or other kinetic moments in his cinema, Hitchcock's cinema was never graphic (again, the Production Code didn't allow it for most of his film-making career), and his violence was sparing, used as punctuation in movies built around suspense. Hitchcock's films are chilling, not just because they show us evil unloosed into the world, but because that evil is so often banal and everyday, walking around on the streets of a town or city just like ours.

The very same kind of evil that might even be within us.

We'd like to believe that evil lies out there, outside our families, outside our country, even, but the unfortunate truth was beautifully stated by the writer G. K. Chesterton when he was asked by the *London Times* to contribute an article on what was wrong with the world.

"Dear Sirs," he wrote.

"I am."

The apostle Paul said that we could not imagine that we were pure and only others were evil, "for all have sinned and come short of the glory of God."[25]

But we'd certainly like to think this, which explains the power of scapegoating, finger pointing, and the unexamined life—and the discomfort we receive from some stories that suggest we, too, as individuals, religious groups, or nations, may be guilty of the worst impulses.

Throughout his career, Hitchcock made a point of creating not just appealing heroes played by leading actors and actresses, but also of presenting appealing and sympathetic villains. In a conversation with Hitchcock, screenwriter Ernest Lehman, who wrote *North by Northwest* and Hitchcock's last picture, *Family Plot*, Lehman made the mistake of asking if the audience would root for the villains.

"Of course!" a surprised Hitchcock replied.[26]

Through our involvement with their characters, and through cinematic legerdemain, Hitchcock even contrived to implicate us in the evil his villains commit. In Hitchcock's favorite of his films, *Shadow of a Doubt*, we meet Uncle Charlie (Joseph Cotton), a handsome and charming man beloved by his sister and niece—and also a cold-blooded murderer known as the Merry Widow Killer. *Rear Window*'s murderer (Raymond Burr) ultimately proves to be a downtrodden sad sack who almost makes James Stewart's Jeff seem in the wrong when he asks why Jeff is dogging his steps: "Do you want money? I don't have any money." *North by Northwest* features the refined and cultured James Mason as its villain, Vandamm.

And then there is *Psycho*.

It's impossible to reproduce today the shock that this movie created when it came out. Just as everyone now knows that "Rosebud" was the sled, we all know that the nervous and soft-spoken Norman Bates (Anthony Perkins) is actually a murderous lunatic.

But to audiences sitting down to the film in 1960, things were very different indeed, and they still can be when we set aside our knowledge and simply watch the movie. Hitchcock actually manipulates us throughout: Our initial sympathy is given to a thief on the run, Marion Crane (Janet Leigh). Although she has stolen $40,000 from her boss's office, it seems justified. She's an attractive character, she needs the money so that her boyfriend can afford to marry her, and besides, she's the star of the movie. Hitchcock cements our attachment to her by placing her in scenes of looming danger—such as when she finds a police car in her rearview mirror—and although we know her theft is wrong, Hitchcock still has us firmly on Marion's side when she pulls up to the deserted Bates Motel, where she meets the quiet and diffident Norman.

Then, slowly, Hitchcock begins to shift our point of view—our attachment—from Marion to Norman. Just before the famous shower scene, Hitchcock shows us Norman looking through the hole he's made in the wall between the office and Marion's room— and then cuts to a camera angle in which we are seeing from Norman's point of view. This editing trope—a character seeing, then our seeing what he sees—puts us in the very mind of the character. An exchange with Lehman as they worked on *Family Plot* shows us that this was how Hitchcock, too, thought about enforcing audience identification:

> **H:** I think we ought to put the audience . . . into the congregation.
>
> **L:** You mean the point of view of the audience?
>
> **H:** Yes.

Then comes the horrific murder—Marion is brutally slain by Norman's mother (we think), and although Norman is a little weird, he's the only logical person left for us to shift our allegiance to. That's how Hitchcock manipulates us into the tortuous scene in which the audience both cheers for Marion's car to sink into the swamp so that he can finish cleaning up the damage done by "Mother" (we're cheering for Norman to cover up a brutal killing) and groans because Marion's money is also going to sink (we're groaning because a lot of stolen money is going to go to waste).

In this and other scenes throughout his canon, Hitchcock indicts us as participants in what we're viewing onscreen, "making the spectator an accomplice, and not merely a witness."[27] He dearly loved the idea of putting the audience in the action, involving us in what we were watching. So like Jeff and Lisa in *Rear Window*, we are implicated as voyeurs peeping into other lives; like the murderous passengers in *Lifeboat*, we approve of the murder of the U-boat captain; like the killers in *Rope*, we sweat throughout the movie to see if they're going to get away with stuffing their victim into the trunk off which they're serving their dinner guests. We are torn with ambivalence in *Vertigo,* split between our desire to see Jimmy Stewart transform shop girl Judy (Kim Novak) into his lost love Madelyn (also Novak)—into an object of his desire instead of a breathing person—and our fear that he will discover that Judy is an accessory to the murder of the "real" Madelyn. In *Suspicion*, we even watch Cary Grant going up the stairs to deliver his wife a glass of milk we think may be poisoned, and all the while we're thinking, "Well, maybe he is a murderer. But he's also Cary Grant, so at least he's a charming one."

So to recap: we are Peeping Toms, participants in a woman's degradation and disintegration, and accessories to murder. Several murders, actually.

It's a pretty impressive rap sheet for just sitting around watching movies.

We do find relational sin in Hitchcock's films (the lovers who kill their friend in *Rope*, for example), as well as societal (the unidentified American governmental agency that forces Eva Marie Saint to prostitute herself so that she can get Vital Information on the Godless Reds in *North by Northwest*). But Hitchcock makes individual evil his primary focus, with the intent of advancing the idea that evil may be monstrous, but it certainly isn't alien.

Sin and evil aren't out there somewhere and brought into the human realm by some *other*, some supernatural being, some stranger. Despite our stereotypes of Hitchcock and his work as "scary," there are no supernatural creatures in his films. No. Evil is a human and familiar thing, and it lurks within the most normal and attractive of us. It's no surprise that two of America's most beloved and iconic actors, Grant and Stewart, appeared in four Hitch films apiece—or that in each film he subverted their usual film personae to implicate them (and us) in sin and evil. By showing us how easily we can be caught up in the actions of these characters, good and bad, Hitchcock pushes us to consider our complicity. It's an important lesson—maybe we can stare down a serpent, turn down a guy with horns and hooves—but sometimes, real evil is seductive because it looks like a normal guy in a bow tie. Or smoking a pipe.

Or taking care of his family.

The Attraction of Evil

Francis Ford Coppola's *The Godfather* traces the ascent of Michael Corleone (Al Pacino) to success in his chosen field. That's the American way, right? Only here, it is actually a descent. As in the films of Alfred Hitchcock, *The Godfather* features attractive, loving, and sympathetic characters played by Pacino, Marlon Brando, Robert Duvall, and James Caan who just happen to be violent, dishonest, and murderous.

The first three and a half minutes of *The Godfather* are one of the great character introductions in American cinema, but there is more than character being presented in this long slow camera movement back from the speaking Bonasera (Salvatore Corsitto) to the viewing angle of the listening Don Vito Corleone (Brando). The movie begins in total darkness—where it will ultimately leave us—and with Bonasera's words: "I believe in America." What the beginning of the movie tells us is that this is going to be a dark film—and that it is going to revolve in some sense around the myth of America. The conjunction of those two—that one can come to America, take care of one's family, be a success in the family business, and yet commit dark and horrific acts—is the foundation of this film, and the fall (for there is no other theological term that has the necessary gravitas) of Michael Corleone from decorated WWII veteran, a man who tells his girlfriend at he beginning of the movie, "That's my family. . . . It's not me," to a cold-blooded murderer and the next don of the Corleone crime family implicates all of us. Michael ultimately takes care of his family and achieves success *because* he is willing to do evil.

But that first scene sucks us in. The camera movement and imperious movement of Don Corleone show his immense dignity and personal power, particularly in contrast to Bonasera, who can't seem to get anything right except his desire for vengeance against the men who brutally beat his daughter. Vito even seems to us a moral character when in response to Bonasera's request for murder, he replies, "That is not justice. Your daughter is still alive."

When at last they reach accord—that the Corleone family will have the men badly beaten, that these "animals" will "suffer as she suffers," Don Corleone asks Bonasera to "accept this justice" as a gift on his daughter's wedding day, and we are goners. This man is powerful, noble, he loves his family. And what could be wrong with justice?

In fact, the first twenty-six minutes of the film, which alternate between scenes of the dimly lit office where Vito hears petitioners on the wedding day of his daughter Connie (Talia Shire) and the bright colors and riotous music of the wedding, show us a group of people we like and admire. Although there have been some discordant notes—such as when Michael tells his girlfriend Kay (Diane Keaton) about the time his father held a gun to a guy's head to release his godson from an unjust contract—on the whole, the Corleones represent a romantically appealing notion of family and life. Vito in fact has told that godson, singer Johnny Fontane (Al Martino), that "a man who doesn't spend time with his family can never be a real man." Vito postpones the taking of the wedding pictures so that Michael can be in them—family isn't family unless everyone is present—and at the end of the wedding sequence, when he takes daughter Connie onto the dance floor, she throws her arms around his neck as he sweeps her away.

The Corleones believe in family values.

Except, of course, that after that first half hour, we begin to find out what the family does to be able to afford such a perfect wedding.

Tom Hagen (Duvall), the Irish orphan taken in and raised by the Corleones, has grown up to be the family's lawyer and counselor, and he flies out to the coast to get Johnny a starring role in Jack Woltz's new movie. When Woltz (John Marley) won't fold, the film mogul wakes, amid satin sheets, to blood—and to the severed head of his beloved race horse Khartoum.

It only takes us a few minutes, then, to discover who these people are—and yet, by then, we're already hooked. Throughout the negotiations with the heroin dealer Sollozzo (Al Lettieri), and the assassination attempt on Vito, our sympathies are still very much with the Corleone family, although we do begin to see a change in Michael. When his family is threatened, he seems to become a different person. After reading the headline about his father's shooting, Michael charges across the street to a phone booth and leaves Kay standing outside in the street, shut off, a powerful foreshadowing for the movie's end. While Kay seems to represent decency and goodness appropriate for an All-American veteran, she cannot go where Michael needs to go to become the Don.

Michael goes to his parents' house, sits in on war councils. After he's beaten up by a rogue police captain on Sollozzo's payroll, he sits calmly, deliberating as Tom and their brother Sonny (Caan) debate strategy. Sollozzo wants Michael to meet with him and help broker a peace; should they choose negotiation or all-out war? Michael says he'll meet with Sollozzo. And then, coolly, calmly, he tells them that if they can get him a gun, he will kill Sollozzo and his police bodyguard.

Sonny laughs. His brother is a war hero. A clean-cut kid. But he's changed, and he has thought the implications through. It's not about the police captain hitting him. In fact, "it's not personal," he tells Sonny. "It's strictly business."

Strictly business. As though that makes murder more palatable somehow. But business is the reason given for many of the violent actions taken in the movie. It wasn't personal, Sollozzo tells Tom after he tries to have Vito killed for refusing his offer. It was strictly business, the traitorous Tessio (Abe Vigoda) tells Tom after he tries to betray Michael.

What are we willing to do for business?

Michael does shoot the men as they sit eating, then he is forced to flee to Sicily as his family buckles down to face the resulting onslaught. In sunny Sicily, Michael meets a beautiful and innocent young girl named Apollonia, woos her, and weds her. It seems like true love. But then, the other mobs strike back, killing Sonny in America and planting a bomb in Michael's car that kills Apollonia in Sicily.

The middle section of the film has always been problematical;

many viewers are outraged and saddened when the snake of sin comes into this Old World Eden and brings Apollonia's death. But the snake was already in the garden. Michael has killed without remorse, and his actions have consequences—if sin brings evil and death into the world, then it is Michael who is ultimately responsible for Apollonia's death. "Apollonia" is a female derivative of the name of the God of the Sun, Apollo, and the Sicilian countryside is always depicted as bathed in sunlight, while Michael has become a creature of darkness. How can Michael's sins survive in the light of day?

"Apollonian" is also, ironically, a word referring to the rational, ordered, and self-disciplined aspects of human nature. We often think of sin as something Dionysian—that comes out in wildness and passion. But Michael is a plotter, a planner, a sinner with forethought.

The most chilling sequence in *The Godfather* is the masterfully edited christening scene in which Michael stands as godfather for the son of a man he intends to murder, his brother-in-law. The scenes of the baptismal liturgy alternate with scenes of Michael's men planning and carrying out the bloody murders of his rivals in New York and Las Vegas. Michael proclaims his belief in the Apostle's Creed, in God: Father, Son, and Holy Spirit. And then, speaking for his nephew and godson, also named Michael, he answers the priest's questions:

"Do you renounce Satan and all his works?"

"I do renounce them," Michael says.

Intercut with this exchange, and in a chilling counterpoint to Michael's words, Coppola shows us five of the Corleone's rivals being gunned down, presumably at the precise moment Michael is taking this solemn oath.

"Will you be baptized?" the priest asks.

"I will."

The water for baptism is then counterposed to images of the flowing blood of the executed, and our understanding of Michael's sacrilege is complete. The godfather relationship is described as a sacred one, but Michael has taken these vows only to screen his plans to kill those who stand in his way or have hurt his family; he has made vows to God and broken them at them same moment, seemingly without remorse.

In the movie's final scene, when Kay, now his wife, comes to him and asks if it is true that he had his sister's husband killed—if he in fact killed the father of his godson—Michael tells her no.

No.

He says it with conviction, solemnly. He is not the man she fears he is.

She is filled with relief. And then, as she watches Michael's men kiss his hand and call him godfather, she and we realize the truth: that the decent man we met at the beginning of the movie has disappeared, and what is left in his place is a killer. Like Anakin Skywalker in the *Star Wars* saga, Michael Corleone may have been sucked into evil acts initially by his concern for his family, but by the time we reach the conclusion of *The Godfather II*, he has given up everything except the desire to succeed. He loses his family. He even kills his brother Fredo—and it's just business.

Business that begins here.

Family business, of course. *American* business. But it is, ultimately, business he chooses for himself.

Jesus once said, "Those who want to save their life will lose it, and those who lose their life for my sake will save it. What does it profit them if they gain the whole world, but lose or forfeit themselves?"[28]

By the end of *The Godfather*, Michael Corleone has become an American success story and lost his soul in the process.

Next, we come to the greatest villain of all, according to the American Film Institute, a man whose cold-blooded deeds chill us because at the same time he exemplifies so much of what we consider to be elevated and refined. If Dr. Hannibal Lecter (Anthony Hopkins) is cultured and humane, a lover of Bach, a gifted visual artist, and a member of the healing professions—and he is—then what are we to make of his calm statement that "A census taker tried to test me once. I ate his liver with some fava beans and a nice chianti."

Human beings don't do that to each other—but then, we might think that they don't send other human beings to concentration camps, or build weapons of mass destruction, or rape women and children as an act of war, and yet these things have happened—and continue to happen—every day. Hannibal Lecter chills us because he is evil—and yet, he is still recognizably human.

As portrayed by Anthony Hopkins, Lecter is a man capable of self-control and gentility. When we first meet Hannibal Lecter, in *The Silence of the Lambs*, he is standing calmly in the middle of his cell at the Baltimore asylum for the criminally insane as though he had been waiting for Agent Starling (Jodie Foster) all his life. He first helps Starling because he can't stand that a fellow inmate of the asylum has been discourteous to her.

But that civility and self-control make his vile and violent acts that much more evil; we'd like to imagine that people lose control and then do something horrible. But when Lecter escapes from prison by beating his guards to death, he does so deliberately, methodically, to the ever-so-civilized music of Bach's *Inventions*. And the Baltimore hospital administrator, Dr. Chilton (Anthony Heald), tells Starling about Lecter's horrific act of violence against a nurse at the asylum: "The doctors managed to reset her jaw, more or less, and save one of her eyes. His pulse never got over eighty-five, even when he ate her tongue."

The hideous basement of the serial murderer Starling is tracking and the self-storage garage where Starling finds her first clue give us scenes that remind us of hell, rendered by Doré, of images by Goya and Bosch; Satan would be at home here. Thomas Harris, the author of the Lecter novels, gives his hideous killers including Lecter some interpersonal and psychological "reasons" for their deviance. The subtext throughout *The Silence of the Lambs*— that Starling is fighting against a culture that commodifies and objectifies women even to the point of killing and skinning them to make a "woman suit"—gives us cultural reasons for some of the evil we witness.

But, ultimately, there is simply Lecter, a personal evil that cannot be adequately explained and cannot be ignored. The reason Lecter is the top movie villain of all time is because we can't put him out of our heads. "They don't have a name for what he is," Starling says at one point, although, unfortunately, *we* do.

Human.

Whether or not we believe in Augustine's formulation of original sin, there seems little question that in this broken world, evil is real and humans are sinful, that even though we may wish to do good we are capable of doing great harm, that it is easier to be bad than to be good. *The Book of Common Prayer* says that although we are made in God's image, "from the beginning, human beings have misused their freedom and made wrong choices. . . . We rebel against God, and put ourselves in the place of God."[29] Hannibal Lecter treats Clarice Starling with courtesy; he may even, in some way, care for her. *Poetry* magazine, his drawings, and a tape recorder playing Bach may lie on top of his desk. He may be capable of incredible insights into people, art, ideas.

But as Lecter himself suggests, "Read Marcus Aurelius. Of each particular thing, ask: What is it, in itself, what is its nature?" Lecter's nature is *human.* He is capable of great good. He is capable of great evil.

As are we all. Another cultured and sympathetic cinematic mass murderer, this one in Steven Spielberg's *Munich,* says, "I think anyone is capable of anything." In *Munich,* and another challenging Spielberg work, *Schindler's List,* we can see the full spectrum of evil emerging—the personal, the interpersonal, and the suprapersonal. We can see that we are enmired in our natures, sinful, prone to violence and exploitation, and that our relationships and systems can sometimes pull us into sin as well.

Evil in the Works of Steven Spielberg

When Oskar Schindler (Liam Neeson) first appears in *Schindler's List,* we know almost as much about him as we are ever going to. Steven Spielberg's camera draws in close to his activities as Schindler gets ready for an important night on the town: picking out a tie, pulling on a coat with a flourish, pulling money from various drawers and hiding places, and, lastly, pinning a swastika on his lapel. Schindler is a German in conquered Poland, a member of the Nazi Party, and a war profiteer out to make a bundle in Krakow.

When he enters the Judenrat, the Jewish Administration Building, at the beginning of the movie to seek the accountant Itzhak Stern (Ben Kingsley), Schindler brusquely walks past the massive queue of Jews that stretches down the street, up the stairs packed with waiting Jews, and into the besieged office full of desperate Jews, newly subjected to the Nazis' debasing rules and regulations. And these Jews, they get out of the way. Schindler looks like—and walks like—a conqueror.

Schindler has come to Itzhak Stern for financial advice, and for help in raising capital so that he can make money. When he asks Stern about a certain formerly Jewish-owned factory for which Stern used to keep the books, Schindler says, "Once the war ends, forget it, but for now it's great, you could make a fortune. Don't you think?" And although Stern tells him that right now his people have other things on their minds than making fortunes, at this point in the story Schindler honestly can't imagine what they might be.

Schindler's List, considered by many people to be Spielberg's masterpiece, is a compelling study of sin and evil on many levels. While we see no supernatural temptation—the only whiff of the supernatural in *Schindler's List* comes when the movie's supreme villain, Amon Goeth (Ralph Fiennes) tries to shoot a Jewish rabbi in the head and first one, then another pistol misfires, again and again—the movie displays individual evil, relational evil, and ultimately, systemic evil, and each of these dramatic depictions of sin can teach us something about the power of evil working in our own lives.

Individual evil is everywhere, of course. If sin is the placing of our own wills ahead of the will of God for us, of our own desires over those of others, if, as Paul Tillich would have it, sin is "estrangement from that to which one belongs—God, one's self, one's world," then that estrangement is initiated in *Schindler's List* by greed, the lust for power, and the loss of self-control.[30]

Oskar could easily represent the first of these, and for part of the movie, he does. He first employs Jews in his factory not because he knows that they are oppressed, but because they are cheaper than Poles. In the wrenching scene in which Krakow's Jews are rousted from their homes and forced to stuff themselves into the ghetto, Spielberg intercuts scenes of crowds taunting a certain family of Jews taken from their comfortable home and their move into crowded quarters in the ghetto, with scenes of Schindler moving into their home, looking around, and, at last, lying comfortably atop the bed, his comfort gained by the suffering of others.

Oskar, of course, changes, although the movie never tells us precisely why. His counterpart, however, the SS officer Amon Goeth, marks his first day as commandant of the Plaszow camp by having a Jewish engineer shot for arguing with him, and Amon never changes, going ultimately to the noose with a "Heil Hitler!" on his lips, and it is Amon Goeth who provides us with our clearest example of personal evil, of a damned human soul. Like Schindler, Goeth is greedy. In their early negotiations, Spielberg has framed them in chairs facing each other, mirror images, as they joust about Schindler's factory and his workers. Later in the film, Spielberg actually intercuts shots of the two men shaving to suggest how many similiarities there might be between these two men, both failed Catholics with failed marriages who were even born in the same year.[31] (Roger Ebert suggests that *Schindler's List* is "two parallel character studies—one of a con man, the other of a psychopath.")[32] The similarities between Schindler and Goeth are important, so that we can learn from the differences.

Like Schindler initially, Goeth wants to squeeze every pfennig he can out of the war, and in his desire to make money, he is not so different from many people. Many of us continue to acquire long after we need to do so, and although we may not personally exploit, terrorize, and kill to do it, there is a similar disconnect in our own lives between our needs and our desires. In *Chinatown*, Jake Gittes (Jack Nicholson) asks the movie's phenomenally wealthy antagonist questions that might be as pertinent to us as to cinematic villains: "Why are you doing it? How much better can you eat? What can you buy that you can't already afford?"

However, Amon doesn't just crave money. He also craves power—one night, he tells Schindler how much he admires him for his ability to remain sober and in control: "That's power," he says. And even more than Schindler, he holds a position of power over the Jews, carries an almost godlike power of life and death. When

Amon sits on the balcony of his villa with a sniper's rifle, he might was well be Zeus raining down bolts from Olympus. Sometimes we see him shooting people for what seems to be a reason—a worker who has stopped to tie her shoe, a worker resting on steps. Goeth, Thomas Keneally's nonfiction novel tells us, was drawn to make targets of idlers and "people of presence," like the engineer or the rabbi he had attempted to kill.[33] But his maid, Helen Hirsch (Embeth Davidtz), tells Schindler that there is ultimately no logic to Amon's exercise of power:

> The more you see of the Herr Kommandant, the more you see there are no set rules you can live by. You cannot say to yourself, "If I follow these rules, I will be safe."

Ultimately, Amon's great evil becomes evident not just because of his greed or his willingess to exercise power selfishly, but because there is no logic or reason to it, no ability to control himself. A heavy drinker, sexually omnivorous and voracious, Amon does violence indiscriminately, beats his maid Helen because of his own attraction to her, and, although the movie catalogs many of his failures of self-restraint, they are only the merest hint of the terrors he actually perpetrated on others. Oskar at one point appeals to Goeth's vanity by telling him that real power is demonstrated by showing mercy, like an emperor pardoning some unworthy wretch who deserves death. The idea appeals to Goeth at first—he manages to pardon several people he would previously have shot or turned the dogs upon—but ultimately he doesn't have the willpower. After a Jewish boy fails to get his tub clean, Amon Goeth shoots him, and he never attempts restraint again.

Although *Schindler's List* powerfully and repugnantly demonstrates personal sin, we can find relational sin in the film as well. The men of the SS are colleagues in degrading and doing violence to the Jews, and as is too often the case with soldiers, their solidarity and common experience sometimes leads them to fraternal sins they would not contemplate on their own or in peacetime. *The Sunflower*, a memoir by Holocaust survivor and Nazi hunter Simon Wiesenthal, records the confession of an SS soldier who had gone along with the atrocities his unit committed—a personal failure, certainly, but one prompted by relationship.[34]

The soldiers, doctors, and associates of the SS—and the structures in place for the "Final Solution" of the "Jewish Problem"—reveal a final level of sin, that of the structural or systemic sin. Peter Gomes has called this "social sin . . . the sinful, fallen nature of the institutions and social systems that are created, managed, and manipulated by sinful men and women."[35] People involved in such institutions may thus do evil, unknowingly or as a result of acquiescence to the terms of their membership in them. Officers or employees may behave unjustly in the pursuit of a corporation's goals—Thoreau wrote that "a corporation has no conscience"—as may the leaders and citizens of a nation in pursuing its aims.[36]

In *Schindler's List*, those systems may seem purely bureaucratic—witness the procedures for registering incoming country Jews shown at the movie's beginning as the Nazi bureaucrats lay out the tools of their trade, the stamps, blotters, and paper on their folding tables—and can even at times be faintly humorous, as in the minor functionaries' references to the sanctity of the list—"The list is correct, Sir"—when Stern is accidentally loaded aboard a cattle car bound for nowhere.

But we can see the dark means to which this system is being put immediately following Stern's rescue from this Kafkaesque bureaucratic nightmare. The camera follows the suitcases of all those loaded on those trains he has just escaped as the suitcases are hauled off into warehouses and dumped, since the owners will never need possessions again. The valuables are taken, piled, or filed. And toward the end of the scene, one of the Jewish workers who is sorting gold has a stack of horror dumped upon his table: recently pulled teeth with gold fillings. Although Schindler walks away from this encounter with the list unknowing, we now know that this is what the system is for, why the trains run, how those incinerators are filled. This is why Rudolf Hoss (Hans-Michael Rehberg), the commandant of Auschwitz, a death camp that could kill ten thousand people a day, every day, could tell Schindler, who has come there to rescue his female workers, "It is not my task to interfere with the processes that take place down here."

Processes.

We regularly cite the Nazis and their "Final Solution" as a geno-cidal oddity that stands as a sort of unique example of societal sin. Certainly Americans are not involved in this sort of evil, simply because they are Americans, right? And yet, as Rowan Williams observes, whenever state violence begins to take innocent lives, it faces the charge that it is no different morally than any violence that takes innocent lives.[37] Does the death of innocents in Iraq stick to our hands? It is this question as to whether societal sin can cause personal evil that is the primary subject of another of Steven Spiel-berg's greatest films, *Munich*.

Like *Schindler's List*, *Munich* is a fictional film based on his-torical events, in this case the 1972 massacre of eleven Israeli Olympic athletes at the Munich games at the hands of an Arab ter-rorist group, Black September, and the later Israeli reprisals for that act. Avner (Eric Bana) is a former soldier and the leader of the group of Israeli assassins we follow through the story as they attempt to kill a group of Arab targets. As their path becomes increasingly dangerous, their moral footing also becomes increas-ingly shaky, so that the clear desire to avenge the Israeli athletes becomes a bog that may cause all of them to be lost. Ty Burr, who called *Munich* Spielberg's finest film in years, noted that "you can take it as both a stunningly well-made international thriller and a drama of deepening moral quicksand."[38]

It is either a great irony or a tragedy, depending on your view-point, that *Schindler's List* and *Munich* should stand as Spielberg's bookend meditations on the destructive power of the state, since one concerns the near-obliteration of the Jews in Europe at the behest of the state and one concerns Jews sent to Europe to kill their enemies at the behest of the state. *New York Times* critic Manohla Dargis wrote that *Munich* was "an unsparingly brutal look at two peoples all but drowning in a sea of their own blood," and argued that it was "by far the toughest film of the director's career and the most anguished."[39]

The anguish driving *Munich* comes from two central moral questions: In seeking violent revenge, does the Israeli government become an entity no better than those that have tried to destroy it?

And in serving the dictates of their government, do the agents of the team headed by Avner (Eric Bana) become agents of injustice in danger of losing their souls?

Munich tries to be evenhanded with this volatile and timely topic, but it nonetheless opens avenues of exploration that some of us would prefer to see closed in these post-9/11 days when, we are told, everything has changed. In fact, prime minister Golda Meir (Lynn Cohen) tells Avner that what happened in Munich changed everything, and in a startling reminder of our own responses to 9/11 asks if law even protects people like those who have done the violence.

Certainly the violence done by the Palestinean terrorists to the Israeli Olympic athletes was horrific; many of us remember the attacks, and as viewers, we see flashbacks to the massacre at the Olympics throughout the movie. But the violence Avner's team does is also horrific, and Spielberg never allows us to forget that these are real people being killed by real people. The first murder that Avner and his team perform is of an Arab target who is also a poet; they kill him after he returns home from a reading of his new translation of *The Arabian Nights*. It is an unlovely murder, with nothing clean or simple about it.

So is the next one, the assassination by bombing of a target who happens to have a young daughter. The team fails to see her reenter the building, and when they call the phone they have stuffed with explosives, she answers instead of her father.

It is a scene worthy of Hitchcock in both its craft and its moral ambiguity: Clearly we don't want to see this little girl die, and only good fortune prevents them from detonating the explosive when she answers. But would we be nearly so upset watching this scene if the possible target were the girl's father or another character? What does that say about us as viewers?

The violence continues, and even escalates. In one bombing, the target is killed, but a newlywed husband and wife who had been in the next room are also badly injured and Avner is right there to witness it. In another mission, a target's wife is shot. Innocents as well as targets are being killed in the process of their mission, and it wears on Avner and other members of the team. And what if these targets are not authentic targets?

In other words, what if killing them will change nothing?

Finally, one of the team members, Robert (Matthieu Kassovitz), draws a line for himself when they prepare to board a train to go and avenge one of their own number who is killed. "All this murder comes back to us," he says. "We're Jews, Avner. We don't do wrong because our enemies do wrong."

Echoing his prime minister, Avner responds that they can't afford to be that decent any more, but Robert says, "Suffering thousands of years of hatred doesn't make you decent. We're supposed to be *righteous*. . . . If we lose that, that's everything."

Munich, like *Schindler's List*, is a harrowing movie to watch. As Avner and his team descend further into the violence and destruction they've been ordered to carry out, we can see the cost to them personally. It is a soul-cost, one that Carl (Ciarán Hinds) indicates when he tells the others that he can keep his sanity only by remembering that despite the work they do, he is still a human being.

Avner becomes gaunt, hollow. "I feel less every day," he says. At the movie's end, he has left Israel and moved to Brooklyn, where he meets with his contact Ephraim as we see the Empire State Building and the UN building across the river behind them.

"Did I commit murder?" he asks Ephraim, seeking proof that every man he killed was involved in Munich.

Ephraim assures him that their targets were good targets and encourages him: "You killed them for the sake of a country you now choose to abandon. The country that your mother and father built. You killed them for Munich. For the future. For peace."

But Avner is inconsolable. "There's no peace at the end of this."

They part with the haunting image of the World Trade Center— the movie, of course, takes place long before the 9/11 attacks—just off center behind them. It is a reminder that Avner's statement about peace, at least, was right. At great personal and spiritual cost to themselves, Avner and his men killed Arab terrorists, the enemies of their society, because they were told to.

But terrorism did not go away, and peace even today looks ever more elusive.

So, to sum up: we are sinners ourselves, who bring death and evil into the world. Our relationships can lead us into sin. Our societies can cause us to sin, perhaps unknowingly, perhaps with all too much awareness.

Where is God in all this?

It's important to notice that in *Schindler's List* and *Munich* alike there is evil—but there is also grace, conversion, the possibility of redemption. After Oskar Schindler sees the girl in the red coat wandering about the massacre in the Krakow ghetto, he realizes finally what the system means—death and destruction for human beings like his Jewish workers, or even *for* his Jewish workers. And bad Catholic though he is, he resolves to fight an evil system.

Here, perhaps, is an answer for theodicy: sin and death have come into creation, often because of our own actions. But in this world we have broken with our sin, there is still the possibility of hope. As Rowan Williams puts it, God "has made the world so that evil choices can't just be frustrated or aborted (where would he stop, for goodness sake? He'd have to be intervening every instant of human history) but have to be confronted, suffered, taken forward, healed in the complex process of human history, always in collaboration with what we do and say and pray."[40] Schindler's example—like the example of many of the heroic characters in the films we've discussed here—shows us how that might happen.

In *Munich*, Avner returns to his wife Daphna (Ayelet Zurer) and daughter, haunted by what he has done and by the violence that prompted it. In a powerful scene criticized by some critics for its juxtaposition of flashbacks of the horrific end of the Munich terrorist standoff with a scene of lovemaking between Avner and his wife, John Williams's soundtrack forms a lament for all the victims of violence—the Israeli athletes, the Palestineans gunned down as they tried to escape, Avner's victims, Avner himself. At the beginning and the end of the movie, Daphna puts her hand over Avner's eyes, but at the end of their lovemaking, she looks directly into his eyes, sees his pain, sees him as he has become, and yet she accepts him, body and soul.

"I love you," she says.

This is a startling and redemptive change from the screenplay by Tony Kushner and Eric Roth, which suggests that Avner turns violent in this last scene of lovemaking as he remembers the violence that has shaped his life. The screenplay's scene ends with both Avner and Daphna alone and terrified, but in Spielberg's final version, grace steps in through Daphna's love, easing Avner's torment and moving him toward the possibility of a new life where he can find wholeness again.

Sin and death are an ever-present reality in all the movies we have discussed in this chapter, as they are in life. But in many of these films—as in life—grace abounds.[41] As William Sloane Coffin was able to say, even in the aftermath of his son's death, "And of course I know, even when pain is deep, that God is good."[42] It is sometimes a dark world, but the light shines in the darkness, and the darkness has not—and cannot—overcome it.[43]

And thankfully, that is where we are headed next—toward the light.

Chapter Four

Grace and Redemption

If the World Is Filled with Evil, How Do We Find Salvation?

Redemption, Conversion, and Grace

I think we discovered in the previous chapter that Oskar Schindler was a sinful man. Not as evil as Amon Goeth, or some of the other thugs, functionaries, and opportunists we met in *Schindler's List*, but still, by his own confession, he was a member of the Nazi Party, a munitions manufacturer, a profiteer of slave labor, a criminal.

Moreover, I suppose we could recall that Schindler was irreligious and immoral. He did not worship God regularly or sincerely (we see him inside a cathedral twice; once when he goes to make contacts with dealers in the black market, since they hang out there, and once when he comes inside a church to tell his wife that he wants to reconcile with her); he caroused with extremely bad company; he drank, he smoked, he cursed, he cheated on his wife, over and over and over again.

In a very real sense, we are talking about a person whose actions have estranged him from his true self, from those around him, and from God. Paul Tillich wrote that "sin is separation," and while Oskar may be surrounded by people, he is also alone, and no amount of alcohol or sex can change that.[1]

So what can?

When the movie begins, Oskar doesn't have any sympathy for—or even awareness of—the plight of the Polish Jews. All he wants to do is make a fortune. Yet ultimately he spends the entire fortune he's made to save the lives of 1,300 Jews at a time when all the other Germans around him were sending Jews off to the gas chambers or cheering as they went.

What happened?

Well, in religious terms, we would say that Oskar underwent a conversion, a life-changing experience that, at least in some ways, redeemed him. William James, in his classic book *The Varieties of Religious Experience*, contends that there are two kinds of conversion. One is self-initiated, "conscious and voluntary": a person decides, "I want to be a better person/mother/Christian/painter/ whatever." The other is "involuntary and unconscious": a person is struck suddenly by an awareness or experience and henceforth sees the world/God/herself in a different way.[2] The two can combine, of course—a seeker may find a sudden insight, a flash of grace that completes that stage of her quest. And a person hit by the thunderbolt of realization may then resolve to do better, to allow that revelation's power to move in her life.

That's how Schindler's conversion comes. Although he has made small movements toward sympathy, it is only after he sees the liquidation of the Krakow Ghetto—and the Red Girl wandering about amid the scenes of terror—that he realizes what putting on that Nazi pin means. His horror galvanizes him to realization; the real Schindler said that no one could hide his head in the sand any more after seeing such a thing as murders carried out in plain sight of children. It also galvanizes him into action; instead of continuing to devote his energy and charm to making a fortune, Oskar Schindler begins using that fortune to bribe Nazi officials, buy food for his workers, and even save some of them from death in Auschwitz. He begins actively sabotaging the war effort—after his workers begin making shell casings, Stern suspects him of changing the calibrations on the delicate machines, and Schindler tells him that if their factory ever produces a usable shell for the German army, he will be very upset.

The point is, from the moment of his conversion on, he becomes a different man. Not, we should notice, a faithful husband, churchgoer, or teetotaler, as some would like.

But in the matter of the highest morality, human life, Schindler becomes a righteous person. He understands what, in the beginning of the movie, he could not—that preserving life is more important than making a fortune.

We don't find many religious conversions at the heart of Hollywood movies, not because religious conversion is not important, but because it doesn't typically make a good story. It works in a movie like *Dead Man Walking*, where the movie's conflict is built around whether Sister Helen (Susan Sarandon) will be able to reach death row inmate Matthew Poncelet (Sean Penn) with her message of God's radical love, but most movies don't set up their suspense around a person's decision to accept grace. All the same, the movies often tell stories of redemption, the Shawshank variety and otherwise, because dramatically, stories do seem to work best when characters are required to change, and we as both filmgoers and spiritual beings are drawn to characters who begin their stories in deep trouble and deep need. So although we'll be looking primarily at nonreligious conversion experiences, I think we'll discover that they all shed light on the action that takes place when a person experiences a life-changing relationship with God.

We often hear a movie or story called "redemptive," but what does that mean, exactly? Theologians use the word *soteriology*, derived from the Greek word for salvation, to talk about the study of redemption, where it comes from, how it happens.

In its simplest terms, we might say that salvation in a world of sin comes when we recover our connection with ourselves, with others, with creation, with God. Oskar's conversion does at least some of these things; after his conversion, he is a person trying to be in right relationship, to pursue what is good rather than what is evil. He does what is right instead of what is easy, as Dumbledore (Michael Gambon) directed Harry to do in *Harry Potter and the Goblet of Fire*. And in the words of the Pauline letters, Oskar is, at least to some extent, a new creation.

In Galatians, Paul wrote that what a person believed was not important; the heated debates in the church at Galatia about whether Christians needed to be circumcised as Jews missed the point, "but a new creation is everything."[3] In the Second Letter to the Corinthians, Paul argued that "if anyone is in Christ, there is a new creation: everything old has passed away; see, everything has become new!"[4]

Salvation is about new life, an affirmation of God's creation and our place in it, but to be "saved" means different things to different Christians. To evangelical Christians, at least since around the time of John Wesley, salvation has meant a life-changing personal encounter with Christ that is usually accompanied by strong feeling and amended life. We see a depiction of this in *Tender Mercies* when Mac (Robert Duvall) is baptized with full immersion in a small church (presumably upon his profession of faith in Christ as his savior) and later asks his stepson, who has also just been baptized, if he feels any different yet.

For sacramental faiths like the Catholic, Anglican, and Orthodox traditions, salvation is something that begins when you are brought into communion with Christ at baptism (as infant Michael Rizzi is baptized at the end of *The Godfather*) and continues through the sacramental life and rites of the church. But however it comes, salvation changes our sinful natures so that we may aspire to be more like Christ and less like our fallen human nature, and so that our actions might begin to reflect our new creation. In either case, Jesus is the agent of salvation for Christians, and his death on the cross and subsequent resurrection the hope of the world.

We've actually seen powerful cinematic pictures of redemption in several of the films we've discussed up to this point. In *It's A Wonderful Life*, we saw how George Bailey undergoes a conversion that convinces him that life is worth living and that, more importantly, *his* life is worth living. His desperate prayer to a God he's not sure he believes in is answered; he is shown the way. In *Signs*, Graham Hess undergoes a conversion that convinces him that there is a God who cares for him, even if that God does not intervene to stop our hearts from breaking. Father Hess prays for help to a God he says he no longer believes in and receives an answer through a new understanding of how God works in the world and how everything matters. Both of these men become new creations: they see the world—and their lives in that world—in a new way.

One of the great stories of redemption in recent American film is that of Jules Winnfield, the character in *Pulp Fiction* to whom we keep returning. Unlike George Bailey and Father Graham Hess, Jules is not praying for help; in fact, like most of us, he doesn't sense that he needs help, caught up as he is in typically American patter about television and fast food. Although his sins are outsize and dramatic—he kills people instead of gossiping about his neighbor—Jules nonetheless stands in for us and for our own fallen natures. All of us need to change; the contrasts in Jules's story just make that need a little more obvious.

While you and I can extend grace to each other, and, I hope, do, theologically speaking, grace is defined as unmerited divine favor. Augustine believed that grace was the tug that directed us toward God, while Aquinas thought grace was infused in Christians through the power of the sacraments. Again, however we explain it, grace is necessary for salvation.

Still, I don't know about you, but it's hard for me to think of someone shooting at me as grace of any sort, although that's precisely what the scene where Jules and Vincent survive a point-blank shooting turns out to be for Jules. In this scene, grace is, in literary and theological terms, "epiphany," the momentary showing forth of what reality really is, how things really work. Rowan Williams uses the word "revelation" to describe events like this and Schindler's horrific epiphany in Krakow about the workings of the "Final Solution," moments that "break existing frames of reference and initiate new possibilities of life."[5] After Jules and Vincent look down the barrel of a gun pointed straight at them, Jules sees that the world operates in a different way than he imagined. God has spared his life for a reason, he believes, and that reason is not to go around killing people.

This moment of revelation, of grace, becomes a moment of conversion for Jules. "To be converted," William James said, is "to be regenerated, to receive grace, to experience religion, to gain an assurance": all of these are phrases that describe a process, either gradual or sudden, in which a soul that had been divided and wrong becomes unified and right.[6] Jules tells Vincent, as they continue their theological discussion in the car, that he's decided to give up the life, that he's seen the light, that maybe Vincent wants to play blind man, but from now on, his eyes are wide open.

In response to this moment of grace, Jules wants to change.

Pulp Fiction is, in fact, filled throughout with examples of grace, unexpected moments when unexpected things happen. Vincent not only saves the life of Mia (Uma Thurman), the wife of his boss Marsellus Wallace (Ving Rhames), but he administers the adrenaline shot to her heart himself. Butch (Bruce Willis) goes back into the basement of a creepy pawn shop to save Marsellus, the very same gangster who has put out a death sentence on him for not throwing a fight. (Later, Butch even rides out of the movie atop a chopper named "Grace" in an escape that's unmerited, if not exactly unearned.) Even filmmaker Quentin Tarantino extends grace, to his characters and to us, his viewers. By breaking up the chronology of the film, Tarantino brings Vincent back to life in the movie's final section even though he's just been filled full of lead in the section preceding.

We love the idea of grace—who doesn't want to be treated better than she or he deserves?—but it can be easily misunderstood, and the idea that we are saved by grace and only by grace, emphasized in the Pauline Epistles and the theology of the Protestant Reformation, has encouraged some Christians to think of grace as something God pours down and we simply receive like kids outside in a rainstorm with our mouths open. Dietrich Bonhoeffer famously railed against "cheap grace," which he described as grace where "no contrition is required, still less any desire to be delivered from sin." If grace does everything, if there is such wonderworking power in the blood of the Lamb, then, many contemporary Christians ask, why should I do anything?[7]

So it's good to see that Jules begins taking necessary steps toward salvation. And what about Vincent and Marvin (Phil LaMarr), who were also witnesses to this revelation? Well, Vincent rejects it entirely, as we've already seen, and unlike Jules, he shortly winds up dead for remaining in his sinful life. "The wages of sin is death," Paul tells us in Romans 6:23, and Vincent gets his wages. But Marvin is an interesting case: When Vincent turns to Marvin, sitting in the back seat, and asks what he thinks about all this miracle and God talk, Marvin tells him, he doesn't even have an opinion.

And at that instant, Vincent's gun goes off—without his pulling the trigger, he swears—and shoots Marvin, killing him.

Apparently you cannot sit on the fence about grace.

So grace is unmerited and sometimes, as in Jules's case, unasked for, but it can't be unwanted. Grace is necessary for salvation, but so is acceptance.

Pulp Fiction allows us to see how Jules's new life begins to change him. When he and Vincent are caught in a coffee shop robbery, his former response would be to kill the robbers, and he could do so easily—although they talk tough, they are, after all, Pumpkin and Honey Bunny (Tim Roth and Amanda Plummer). Instead, although Jules has Pumpkin right in his sights, he tells him to sit down and they'll try and work something out. Usually they'd be dead as fried chicken, he tells them, but they've caught him in a transitional period. "So I don't wanna kill you. I wanna help you."

The difference Jules's conversion has made in him seems most visible when he asks Pumpkin if he reads the Bible, then begins to quote him that verse he says is Ezekiel 25:17 (it's actually a hodgepodge of verses and biblical-sounding language, although a portion of Ezekiel 25:17 does reside herein):

> The path of the righteous man is beset on all sides by the iniquities of the selfish and the tyranny of evil men. Blessed is he, who in the name of charity and good will, shepherds the weak through the valley of darkness, for he is truly his brother's keeper and the finder of lost children. And I will strike down upon thee with great vengeance and furious anger those who would attempt to poison and destroy my brothers. And you will know my name is the Lord when I lay my vengeance upon thee.

We know that this is normally a bad sign. Whenever Jules quotes this verse, it means he's about to ventilate somebody. But, as he tells Pumpkin, that morning he had seen something that got him thinking. He muses about some possible ways he might understand this verse now, trying out several self-serving versions before settling on the one that is most honest as well as most challenging:

"The truth is, you're the weak. And I'm the tyranny of evil men. But I'm trying, Ringo—I'm trying real hard—to be the shepherd."

Jules sees what he has been, and he sees it without sentimentality or avoidance. But now, he also sees how he could be something different—how, in William James's language, his soul that has been divided and wrong might become unified and right. His movement from the realization of grace to the acceptance of it, from revelation to action, is apparent here.

What will happen next? Jules has told Vincent that for the rest of his life he'll just walk the earth, like the character Caine (David Carradine) in the television show *Kung Fu*, helping people and having adventures, until God puts him where he wants him to be. That's all we know. In chapter 5 we'll explore in more detail what adventures converted people might have and where God might want us to be, but there are other aspects of salvation to explore in films we haven't discussed in depth, and we'll turn to those before we talk about walking the earth in the redeemed life.

Redemption as Change

Tracy Lord (Katherine Hepburn) in *The Philadelphia Story* is one of the few great popular film characters in need of redemption who happens to be female. In Hollywood films, women characters often help save men from damnation, but rarely seem to need saving themselves. Interestingly, Hepburn, who appeared on Broadway as Tracy before making the film, was also in need of redemption as a performer. After a string of flops, Hollywood trade magazines were calling her "box office poison," and the script, which showed Tracy transforming from an unforgiving ice queen into a woman of flesh and blood, was designed to both tell a great story and rehabilitate her in the film business. It's not that Tracy should change because she's a strong-willed female, of course, although some contemporary audiences might have seen it that way; I think instead there's something to the continuing complaint that Tracy's lack of forgiveness and judgmental nature keep her from experiencing happiness—and bring unhappiness to others.

Two of my favorite stories about easy judgment and the urgency of forgiveness come from the wisdom of the desert fathers, Christians who lived in solitude in Egypt in the fourth century. Although they were solitary, they were not always alone, and in their interactions with each other, they got on each other's nerves, as all of us do in community. Since they were a religious community, they also felt that sometimes it was necessary to judge each other. In one story, a wise old father (*abba*), Abba Moses, received word that one of the brothers had sinned and a group had gathered to judge him.

He didn't go.

When they sent for him, he got up, found a leaky jug, filled it full of water, and then set out on his way to the gathering.

They saw him coming a ways off, and came out to meet him. I can see their faces, can't you? Their quizzical expressions, their questions: "Abba, what are you doing?"

"My sins are leaking out behind me unseen," he told them, "and yet here I come to judge another's sin."

When they heard these words, they called off the meeting and went to their homes.

At another such meeting, a brother was judged for his sin and thrown out of the gathering by the priest, and the aged Abba Bessarion got up from his seat and followed him out, saying only, "I too am a sinner."

If redemption is about becoming fully human, about connecting with the image of God within us, then Tracy's redemption can only come if she can learn to love uncritically (the sort of love the Greeks called *agapē*, the sort of love with which God loves us) and begin to forgive even those of whom she disapproves or those who have hurt her.

Certainly forgiveness wasn't in evidence with Tracy and her first husband, C. K. Dexter Haven (Cary Grant); he drank too much, and she considered it a weakness, rather than a condition requiring love and support. In fact, along with her fiancé, George Kittredge (John Howard), she considers many things to be weakness. Tracy's lack of forgiveness is ongoing—she has encouraged her mother to throw her father—who may or may not be having an affair with a dancer—out of the house, which Mrs. Lord does, although it becomes clear that it was done very much against her will. When Dexter shows up before her wedding with two "friends" of her brother Junius—actually they're a writer and photographer sent to cover the big society wedding, Mike Connor (James Stewart) and Liz Imbric (Ruth Hussey)—Tracy immediately shows that she hasn't lost her contempt for even the memory of Dexter's alcoholism. "It was disgusting," she sneers.

Tracy Lord—that last name is significant—is often described by other characters as someone who is cold, distant, imperious. She's like some marvelous, distant queen," George tells her, and she acts like it. But in the course of the movie, through her interaction with Jimmy Stewart's Mike Connor in particular, she is converted from statue to human being.

But at first, as always in stories about redemption, it doesn't look very promising.

When Dexter first begins to talk with Tracy, their conversation at last leads him to rebuke her prejudice against any form of weakness, her intolerance because, he says, "you'll never be a first-class human being or a first-class woman until you've learned to have regard for human frailty." In another exchange, this time with her father, Seth (John Halliday), she hears from him that she has everything it takes to make a lovely woman except the one essential: an understanding heart, without which she might as well be made of bronze.

Forgiveness.

It's biblical, you know. We find references to the importance of forgiveness and requests for forgiveness scattered throughout the Hebrew Bible; the history of the people of God seems to be a continuing cycle of sin, repentance, and God's forgiveness. In the new covenant promised by God to Jeremiah, one of the most important passages in the Hebrew Testament, God promises to create a renewed relationship with the house of Israel, to

> put my law within them, and I will write it on their hearts; and I will be their God, and they shall be my people. No longer shall they teach one another, or say to each other, "Know the LORD,"

for they shall all know me, from the least of them to the greatest, says the LORD; for I will forgive their iniquity, and remember their sin no more.[8]

In the New Testament, every Gospel records Jesus' passion for forgiveness, and we are told, flatly, in Matthew, "if you forgive others their trespasses, your heavenly Father will also forgive you; but if you do not forgive others, neither will your Father forgive your trespasses"; in Mark, "Whenever you stand praying, forgive, if you have anything against anyone; so that your Father in heaven may also forgive you your trespasses"; and in Luke, "Do not judge, and you will not be judged; do not condemn, and you will not be condemned. Forgive, and you will be forgiven."[9]

Ouch.

It seems pretty airtight, all right; we are called upon to forgive, anything against anyone at anytime, and we're told our own forgiveness depends upon it. We can't be the person God intends for us to be unless we do. We're not supposed to judge or to condemn, but to pardon.

Oh, but forgiveness is hard—as hard, perhaps, as Tracy Lord. To stand in judgment is not only easier, it's safer. We can never be hurt if we hide behind skin of marble.

But we can never be whole, either.

How does Tracy at last become a new creation? Partly it's in response to confronting a mirror image of her own prejudices. "Man of the people" Mike Connor takes an instant dislike to the Lords as members of the privileged class, and he believes that because Tracy is a rich society bride that she's probably a certain kind of woman with whom he wants nothing to do, young, rich, and rapacious. When he finds her reading stories from his book, he actually tells her that girls like her get in trouble when they read books like his. They begin to *think.*

"That's bad."

And he truly hurts her feelings when she warms to him after reading some of his fiction and offers him the use of her farmhouse in the country to write another book, telling her that the idea of artists depending upon a rich patron went out years ago. Connor's prejudice toward her drops, eventually—particularly after both he and Tracy have had too much to drink—but being judged stirs something in Tracy that makes her angry, even though she doesn't recognize the irony yet.

"You're just a mass of prejudices," she tells him the night before her wedding. "Your intolerance infuriates me! I should think that, of all people, a writer would need tolerance. The fact is you'll never, you can't be a first-rate writer or a first-rate human being—"

And she stops short, hearing Dexter's words to her. The other factor in her conversion is that she gains a new sympathy for weakness by drinking too much at her wedding party and participating with Mike Connor in what she fears might be a serious departure from her rigid morality. Needing forgiveness gives Tracy a new understanding of its importance, and being treated by her fiancé George as she would typically treat others is an eye-opener. When George takes a powder and Dexter offers himself as a replacement groom, she accepts, announces to the entire gathered wedding crowd that she has made a terrible fool of herself—here is change in action—and then she goes to talk to her father:

Tracy: Wait. How do I look?

Seth: Like a queen. Like a goddess.

Tracy: And you know how I feel?

Seth: How?

Tracy: Like a human. Like a human being.

"The time to make up your mind about people is never," is what Tracy has told Mike Connor about his judgment and prejudice— and that is one of the most Christian sentiments I can imagine. When Tracy Lord begins to apply it, she becomes a person truly capable of good.

Like Jules in *Pulp Fiction* and Tracy in *The Philadelphia Story*, Roger O. Thornhill (Cary Grant) in *North by Northwest* also doesn't realize he's lost. How could he? He seems to be as found as a person can get. In the opening moments of the movie he is introduced through his words and actions as a successful and extremely busy executive, totally in command of bustling Manhattan—although he also shows himself to be a vacant and selfish person who dictates a vacuous love note to the latest woman he's dating and steals a cab from an old lady by lying about his secretary's health. During the movie, it is revealed that Roger's middle initial "O" (like that of David O. Selznick, for whom Hitchcock once unhappily worked) stands for nothing. A big fat goose egg. Roger O. Thornhill (the initials, of course, spell "rot") is empty at his core, a big zero in the middle, and although that vacuum may be disguised by his activity and his ability to manipulate his environment, the action of the movie shortly forces Thornhill out of his element, where he can no longer hide from himself.

By casting Cary Grant in this film, Hitchcock was again pushing him, at least initially, to play against his persona. For much of the movie, Roger O. Thornhill doesn't seem much like the heroic Cary Grant, and that's where the notion of redemption lies in *North by Northwest*. Although they disagreed on much, the dueling theologians Pelagius and Augustine could agree on one thing: that human beings bore the imprint of God. Pelagius suggested that newborn infants came into the world bearing the express image of God, while Augustine believed that human beings are stamped with the imprint of God like the imprint of a signet ring in wax.

If, as we said earlier, redemption is indeed about our becoming who God wants us to be, if what redemption means is either rediscovering or reclaiming that image, becoming the creatures we are meant to be, then what redemption means for Cary Grant in *North by Northwest* is becoming "Cary Grant." As charming and handsome as he is from the outset of the film, he is also supremely self-centered, and before he can become the hero we expect him to be, he must give up believing in nothing besides himself and learn how to sacrifice for others.

Roger Thornhill's world turns topsy-turvy when he's mistaken for a nonexistent spy named Kaplan and almost killed, although even when he's in danger, his dialogue with Vandamm, the villain of the piece, shows that he is still self-possessed enough to be ridiculously myopic: "Not that I mind a slight case of abduction now and then, but I have tickets for the theater this evening, to a show I was looking forward to and I get, well, kind of *unreasonable* about things like that."

In an attempt to learn what is happening to him, he winds up framed for murder. When he hops a train to Chicago to escape, he is taken in and hidden by Eve Kendall (Eva Marie Saint), a beautiful and distant blonde for whom he falls hard. Although she is actually trying to help him, Eve hurts Thornhill with her unwillingness to connect. "I want you to leave right now," she tells him. "Stay far away from me, and don't come near me again. We're not going to get involved. Last night was last night, and it's all there was, and it's all there is. There isn't going to be anything more between us. So please. Goodbye, good luck, no conversation, just leave."

It sounds like the sort of thing that Thornhill would say—and probably has said—to women. Like Tracy Lord, Roger Thornhill, when faced with someone who is a mirror image of himself, is forced to look at his own reflection, and finds it lacking

When he discovers that Eve is working for those who want to kill him—it's Eve who, unwillingly, sends Thornhill to that improbable crop-dusting assassination attempt in the Indiana cornfield—he tries to hurt her, but only winds up casting suspicion on her with her employer (and lover) Vandamm—which could be deadly, since Eve is actually a double agent working for the United States and always has been.

When he learns that he has put Eve in danger with his self-centeredness Thornhill steps out of his own inflated ego, his own fear and jealousy and hurt, and begins to feel for someone else. And when he does, he becomes someone else: the Cary Grant we've been waiting for. He allows himself to be shot with blanks to remove suspicion from Eve (it doesn't work), and then he climbs into the cantilevered house on top of Mount Rushmore where she's staying to try to rescue her. Again, it's frightening—Thornhill is now in emotional danger, as well as the obvious physical danger he's daring. But he rescues Eve, and in the process, rescues himself.

Although he had been twice married, and doubtless his selfishness and distance contributed to the failure of those marriages, the end of the movie finds him married to Eve, pulling her up into the bunk of their train compartment just as, at great risk to himself, he stretched out his hand to save her from falling off Mount Rushmore. Roger Thornhill's redemption comes from risking himself for another—which allows him to fill that hollow spot inside himself.

We can see a similar movement from selfishness to redemption in *The Fisher King*, although this movie is explicitly about redemption and about radio personality Jack Lucas (Jeff Bridges) becoming the creation God intends him to be. Early in the film Jack is given a Pinocchio doll that reappears all through the movie, and the story of Pinocchio, a puppet boy who at last becomes a real flesh-and-blood boy, is an obvious analogue for Jack's story and what he needs: to become a real man.

Like Jules Winnfield in *Pulp Fiction*, Jack experiences an unaccountable moment of unlikely grace that sets him back on his heels; like Tracy Lord, he needs to become human; like Thornhill, he ultimately finds redemption through unselfishly helping others. But Jack's story also has a religious and mythic element, because what Jack needs to find is the Holy Grail, the cup of Christ that, in the medieval story of the Fisher King, brings healing to all who drink from it.

And Jack does need healing. At the beginning of the movie, although he, like Thornhill, is empty inside, it's not because he doesn't possess everything that our society tells us will make us happy. Jack has money—we can tell by his elegant apartment. He has power—as a successful shock jock, he can influence people's opinions—too powerfully, it turns out. He's about to get his own TV show, with his own comic catchphrase: "Forgive me." He has a beautiful girlfriend all but imprisoned in his tower. So: money, power, fame, love—and yet Jack is still wounded. Like the rich young ruler who came to Jesus in the Gospel of Luke, Jack seems to have everything—and still, that ruler asked Jesus what he needed to do to be saved.

"Sell all that you own and distribute the money to the poor," was Jesus' answer. "Then come, follow me." And the young man went away still miserable—because he had great wealth, and wasn't willing to give it up. And yet he knew he was losing something in walking away.[10]

Jack has lots of things, but he doesn't have peace, and he becomes more miserable, more wounded, when his comments to a frequent caller to his show spur the man to shoot up a restaurant.

After that, Jack falls off the map for three years. When we find him, he is working in a video store, chronically depressed, living with the video shop's owner, Ann (Mercedes Ruehl), and just an inch or so away from taking his own life. In fact, he's just about to jump into the river with concrete blocks (and the Pinocchio doll) tied to his feet when through a string of events he is rescued from suicide and worse by Parry (Robin Williams), a street person Jack later discovers was driven insane by the murder of his wife—in the shooting spree Jack inspired by his offhand comments on the radio.

Okay then—here is Jack's chance for redemption. I mean, clearly it means something that Parry's path has crossed his, right? Redemption doesn't simply come from the recognition of that grace, however, or from good works that Jack performs from the desire for redemption; Jack must become a new creation. He tells Ann, "I wish there were some way I could just pay the fine and go home," but redemption isn't so easy.

Jack gives Parry some money, asking, "How much is this gonna take?" When Parry gives the money to another homeless guy, Jack raises his eyes to heaven and says, "I just want you to know that I gave him the money." It's not enough of course; it isn't giving of himself, and trying to "pay the fine" doesn't change Jack in any way.

Later, Jack tries to fix Parry up with Lydia, the girl of his slightly-obsessive dreams (Amanda Plummer), and when the evening goes well, he's sure that must be it. The heat is off; good deed accomplished, good karma earned, and Jack hasn't really had to do that much to make it happen. Jack thinks that he is cured, he begins to get his old confidence back, and he falls back into his old life as a radio personality as though the world is fixed.

Only it isn't—when he discovers that Parry is lying in a hospital ward in a coma, Jack cracks. To honestly help Parry, Jack will have to put aside his self-centered ways and perform acts that would be as insane in the eyes of the world as they are in his, the acts of faith that Søren Kierkegaard often called "absurd."

The apostle Paul talks throughout 1 Corinthians about how Christianity and its tenets may seem to be foolishness to outsiders, and writes that "Those who are unspiritual do not receive the gifts of God's Spirit, for they are foolishness to them, and they are unable to understand them because they are spiritually discerned."[11] Parry may be insane—okay, is insane—but earlier he had told Jack about what the Grail means and even where the Grail is, and Jack discerns that whether these are literal truths or not, they are spiritual truths. So Jack breaks into the townhouse Parry showed him, and in the process of taking the "grail" (actually a trophy), he also foils the suicide of another despondent soul. It's an action that doesn't make sense—but it works. Or what works is radical and ridiculous and unselfish love, about which more later.

The story of the Fisher King, who was wounded and wasting away, and the story of Jack's redemption remind me of the desire of Dame Julian of Norwich to be wounded. I mean, who in their right mind wants to be wounded? Don't we normally try to avoid such things? But Julian said that she wanted three wounds: "the wound of true contrition, the wound of loving compassion, and the wound of longing with my will for God."[12]

It sounds like a recipe for redemption—and a good plot synopsis for *The Fisher King*.

Because of his wounds, Jack *has* changed. As in the Grail story Parry tells Jack in detail, the Fisher King has learned from the Fool—and learned, perhaps that he is the fool. After he makes tremendous, self-giving sacrifices so that Parry can be healed, he returns to find Ann, who sits at her desk at the video store, just watching him. Like Pinocchio, there are certain things Jack needs to do to be a real man instead of a puppet, and one of those is to truly love. So when Jack shows up at the video store and haltingly announces, "I love you," it proves the reality of the conversion experience. Jack has indeed changed from the self-centered and totally lost person we met at the beginning of *The Fisher King*, and in the process, he has helped another.

The Power of Love

Saving others isn't always possible, though, as Robert Redford's *A River Runs Through It* demonstrates. Our own redemption and the redemption of others is separate, however we might want to see change in the people we love. Based on the true story of writer Norman Maclean's own Montana family, *A River Runs Through It* is about two brothers who need help and the people who love them and want to save them.

The primary story concerns Norman (Craig Sheffer) and his brother Paul (Brad Pitt), who grow up with their minister father and their mother in the unspoiled Montana of the early twentieth century. Norman goes off to university; Paul stays in Montana and gets into trouble: women, alcohol, gambling, and violence. The police sergeant (MacIntyre Dixon) tells Norman they are picking his brother up too often, and clearly Paul is in over his head.

Lost, we might even say.

Norman wants to help, but how? All he knows is that when they fish, everything seems to be all right. It's how they were raised.

"My father was a Presbyterian minister and a fly fisherman," the Older Norman (Robert Redford himself) says in voice-over at the beginning of the movie. "In our family, there was no clear line between religion and fly-fishing." It's an important clue for us in how to read the movie: spirituality and fishing are going to be closely linked, and the possibility for salvation lies close to the art of fishing. Norman's father in fact believed that "all good things, trout as well as eternal salvation, come by grace, and grace comes by art, and art does not come easy." While all of them are good fishermen, Paul is tremendously gifted, so beautiful in action that his fishing itself is grace and art. It is through fishing that Norman hopes to save his brother; it is also through sending her brother fishing with Paul and Norman that Norman's girlfriend, Jessie (Emily Lloyd), hopes she can save him.

Things don't work out that way. It turns out that Jessie's brother has other things on his mind than fishing, and it almost wrecks Paul and Norman's day together. When Norman wants to desert Jessie's brother, his conversation with Paul, though, reveals truths about both the idea of help, and about Paul. Norman believes that nothing he does can make a difference, but Paul replies, "Maybe what he likes is somebody trying to help him."

Norman and Paul later take another day fishing, along with their father, and as the sun sparkles on the waters, Paul casts miraculously and then athletically lands a big one. (The images in *A River Runs Through It* are worth mentioning in discussing a movie that consciously talks about grace and beauty, since its beauty won it an Academy Award for Best Cinematography.) It's a wonderful day, filled with transcendent moments—and not to be repeated.

Away from the river, you see, Paul can't be saved—or at least, Norman cannot save him. After her brother left Montana, Jessie had asked Norman, "Why is it the people who need the most help won't take it?"

It's a question for which many have us have sought an answer.

When Paul dies, violently and not unexpectedly, it falls to Norman to bring the news to his parents. Afterward, they sometimes puzzle over it, over Paul, and over their failures to save him. Once, Norman tells his father, "Maybe all I really know about Paul is that he was a fine fisherman."

"You know more than that," the dour Scot says. "He was beautiful."

And in one of the last sermons he ever preached, in front of Norman and Jessie and their children, the Reverend Maclean delivers what may be his final conclusion on the matter. Perhaps they cannot save those who desperately need help. "But we can still love them—we can love completely without complete understanding."

Redemption is ultimately a personal matter—and while we might pray, and seek to help, we cannot save another. Only God can save.

But we can love, and that love can be transformational for us— and maybe, God willing—for another. Again, Hollywood doesn't make many movies about how love can make religious transformation possible. But it makes lots of movies about love, and the radical love represented in many Hollywood love stories shows how in some respects, all the clichés are true.

Love changes things.

The Bible has a great deal to say about love—love of parents for their children, of husband for wife, of God, and of God for God's people. "Love" appears 584 times in the Bible. In the Hebrew Bible, we often see the phrase "steadfast love" used to describe God's love for God's people, as is sung in 1 Chronicles, "O give thanks to the LORD, for he is good; for his steadfast love endures forever," or Psalm 86, "But you, O Lord, are a God merciful and gracious, slow to anger and abounding in steadfast love and faithfulness."[13]

But it is in the Christian Testament that love becomes a real sign of transcendence and conversion, in passages too numerous to list here. In each of the Synoptic Gospels (Matthew, Mark, and Luke), Jesus condenses all the commandments of Jewish law into this: love the Lord with heart, mind, soul, and strength, and love one's neighbor as oneself.[14] In the Gospel of John, Jesus' one commandment is for his followers to love each other as he has loved them, and he tells them that there is no greater love than to give their life for each other.[15]

But we are not just called to love one another, the members of the body of Christ: in the Gospels and in the Pauline and Johannine Epistles we are called to love even those we don't want to love, those who are not like us, those whom we might consider enemies. Jesus' parable of the Good Samaritan, a story told in answer to a legalistic question about love, tells us that true love is dangerous, that love is not negotiable, that to be a child of God is to love without reservation, as difficult as that may be.[16] The writer of the letter 1 John puts it this way: "Whoever does not love does not know God, for God is love."[17]

Ah, but what kind of love? For the word "love" has become so debased in our society that we use it interchangeably for God and nail polish. I love my children and I love my iPod, and believe me, although we are using the same word, we are not referring to the same feeling. We talked earlier about the Greek word *agapē*, which is an unselfish love untainted by lust or desire for self-promotion. Paul Tillich (and later Martin Luther King Jr., following his lead) said that *agapē* was a love that "seeks the other one in his center. *Agapē* sees him as God sees him."[18] *Agapē* is a transforming love—that is, it transforms those who experience it, if they choose to be transformed.

And it transforms us.

Disney's *Beauty and the Beast* is a love story built around the need for redemption. In the opening scenes, we hear how a young prince (Robby Benson) was cursed by an enchantress with the form of a beast for being "spoiled, selfish, and unkind" (anyone seeing a pattern here with the selfishness thing?) until such time as a woman could love him. A tall order, as the movie suggests, "for who could ever learn to love a beast?" But as we've seen, what seems ridiculous in the eyes of the world is not ridiculous in God's eyes; as Kierkegaard writes, while much is impossible in the physical realm, "everything is possible spiritually speaking."[19]

Beauty and the Beast is marked by scenes of sacrificial love. When Belle (Paige O'Hara) offers to remain in the Beast's castle to ransom her father, who has wandered into it unknowing, it is a sacrifice that sets the Beast aback: "You'd do that?" he asks. Like Schindler, the thought had never occurred to him, but here Belle is offering us a clear vision of how the Bible speaks about how salvation occurs. Christ, in dying on the cross in perfect obedience to the Father's will, "came not to be served but to serve, and to give his life a ransom for many."[20] The captive is freed, and Belle takes his place.

It is a countercultural message, set up against the supremely egoistic love of the local hero, hunter Gaston (Richard White), who wants Belle because she's the most beautiful, "and that makes her the best." Gaston is the model for his society (and probably also for ours, I fear); his sidekick Lefou (Jesse Corti) sings to Gaston that "everyone's awed and inspired by you," and he's acknowledged as leader and the most eligible bachelor in the village. But Gaston could never see Belle as she is—he doesn't understand her love for books, for example—and like most people, when he looks at the Beast, he sees only a monster. So Gaston is a reminder that what the world loves is not worth emulating; true joy comes, paradoxically, from self-sacrifice.

Throughout the film, Belle, her father, and even the Beast himself, offer themselves in love, offering to sacrifice themselves.

When Belle attempts to escape and finds herself in the forest surrounded by wolves, the Beast defends her, although he is grievously wounded in the process; then Belle, who could leave him and go, brings him back to the castle and tends him, although it means her imprisonment. At last, even though the enchantress's deadline for someone to love the Beast looms, he sees that she is unhappy and needs to aid her father, and releases her from her pledge, even though it means the loss of his happiness, and of any hope of ever being himself. He tells his majordomo, Cogsworth (David Ogden Stiers), that he has let her go. "I had to . . . I love her."

When Gaston leads an attack on the castle to kill the Beast, egocentric love and selfless love meet in battle, and it is Gaston who finally falls into the depths below. The Beast too seems dead, but at Belle's teary profession of love—love for him, for the him he has become during the course of the story—something changes.

In a blinding show of light, the Beast is floated off the ground, rotated slowly—and is at last lowered back to earth, a human prince. It looks very much like the kind of divine intervention in sudden conversion that William James describes: "Throughout the height of it he undoubtedly seems to himself a passive spectator or undergoer of an astounding process performed from above. . . . Theology, combining this fact with the doctrines of election and grace, has concluded that the spirit of God is with us at these dramatic moments in a particularly miraculous way, unlike what happens at any other juncture of our lives. At that moment, it believes, an absolutely new nature is breathed into us."[21]

Conversion is an *ontological* change—that is, it affects the most basic level of our being, who and what we are. Love has changed the Beast (and while we might argue that being turned back into a handsome prince might make anyone lovable, it would be missing the point). Again, redemption is about our turn toward the image of God planted or rediscovered within us, seeking the perfection of what God intends us to be. The handsome prince dancing with Belle at the movie's conclusion is an exterior reflection of the beautiful soul that is now within, unlike the hunky Gaston, who always had the appearance of beauty but who inside was twisted and venomous with self-love and other-hatred.

Love stories in movies tell us about love in general, but one of the reasons they help us understand something about salvation and redemption is that the very act of couples coming together, as they do in love stories and romantic comedies from *It Happened One Night* to *When Harry Met Sally*, from *Charade* to *Ring of Fire*, marks these stories as belonging to the dramatic genre called "comedy." As a genre, comedy is not about funny ha-ha; from the drama of the ancient Greeks to today, it has been about the affirmation of life—that life is worth living and worth continuing, and that this is best represented dramatically by marriage and couples forming to carry on life on the planet. In the religious context we've been examining, comedy affirms creation, and our place in that creation. What the radical hope and love of Hollywood love stories gives us is a firmer understanding of grace and how we might change to live in hope and love.

One final story of conversion that revolves around a love story appears in *Magnolia*, a film we discussed briefly in chapter 1 from the standpoint of belief. *Magnolia*, as we said, features a group of characters who are broken and who need to be whole, who need conversion but are so sunk in themselves and their own loathing and self-loathing that change seems impossible. My favorite of the story lines in the movie revolves around a recently divorced Catholic L.A.P.D. officer, Jim Kurring (John C. Reilly), who falls like a ton of bricks for Claudia (Melora Walters), a truly messed-up woman he meets when he comes to her house on a noise complaint (and interrupts her as she does lines of coke). In the opening montage of the film when all the characters are introduced, Officer Kurring is described for us through his personal phone ad, where he tells us that he has a stressful job and so is looking for someone calm, undemanding, and loving.

Well, Claudia ain't it. Haunted by her molestation by her father, the TV game show host Jimmy Gator (Philip Baker Hall), she has become a self-hating cokehead who hooks up with men to satisfy her drug habit. Like many of the characters in *Magnolia*, she is lost—Lost, even—broken beyond any possibility, we might think, of redemption. References to Exodus are buried throughout *Magnolia*—and not just as a clue to those damn frogs. Writer/director

Paul Thomas Anderson also has characters make references to how
the past is not through with us, how the iniquities of the fathers will
be visited upon the children, and the children's children.[22] It
doesn't seem to be a cycle that can ever be broken.

But, again, what is impossible for man, is not impossible for
God.[23]

When Claudia opens the door to Jim's knock, the camera comes
in on his face to emphasize how stunned he is by what he sees.
After talking with her for a bit, he asks her for a date, and she
accepts. When he leaves the apartment he thinks about her as
someone that God has miraculously put in his life—You've given
me this chance, and I'm not going to screw it up, he tells God at
one point—and although both of them have harrowing days, that
night their date actually seems to be going well. Claudia asks Jim
if they can agree not to pretend with each other, if they can agree
to be who they really are—but when Jim agrees, Claudia begins to
get cold feet.

Here is a person who listens to her, a person who is willing to
be himself with her, a person who sees her—and who could see her
as she really is.

Only, Claudia doesn't like the person she really is. In fact, many
of us think that no one could love us as we really are, but fortunately *agapē* doesn't work like *eros* or *philia*, types of love that
have romantic or friendship connotations; it's not about our worth,
perceived or understood. The Gospel of Mark's rendering of Jesus'
talk with the rich young ruler tells us that Jesus looked at the young
man and loved him.[24] This wasn't a love based on what the ruler
could do for Jesus; it was a love that saw him as he was, and as he
could be, and that loved him in spite of all.

Claudia can't imagine that anyone could ever look past her
addiction and her messed-up soul and love her in that way—or that
anyone else would admit to being messed-up too. At dinner, she
tells Jim that she is nervous that once he really gets to know her he
won't like her. And when he confesses his secret fear—that
although he seems so together, he really isn't either—she is
stunned.

It is great—and it's frightening. Be careful what you ask for.

"Now that I've met you," she asks Jim, "would you object to never seeing me again?"

And then, in tears, she dashes out of the restaurant.

She runs away, afraid to love and be loved, and it's a sentiment that Jim Kurring could probably identify with at the moment. As a divorced Catholic, his failure in love has cut him off from his faith tradition; as someone who has just been left sitting alone at the table by the first woman he's asked out in the two years he's been single, he probably feels hurt and humiliated. But, as you may remember, something miraculous happens in *Magnolia*: frogs fall from the heavens.

In almost all of the story lines in *Magnolia*, that divine intervention pushes people who were about to come off the tracks back onto them, some more securely than others, and that's what seems to happen with the characters in this story, Jim especially. After he leaves the restaurant Jim finds himself helping a robber (William C. Macy), who has pathetically bungled a theft, return his ill-gotten gains, and then he listens to him talk about why he did it: in a roundabout way, it's because he wants to love someone. "I really do have love to give. I just don't know where to put it."

Jim knows where to put it. When he gets into his car, he drives back to Claudia's house. And there in the apartment, in the bedroom where we earlier heard Claudia screaming at her father to get out, to get away from her, Jim tells her that he wants to do what she asked him in the restaurant:

> Whatever you wanna tell me, whatever you think might scare me, won't . . . I won't judge you . . . you shouldn't be scared of scaring me off or anything that you might think I'll think or on and on and just say it and I'll listen to you . . .

Magnolia is, as we saw earlier, a film about how what seems to be merest chance or happenstance may actually be part of some larger will for creation. Officer Jim Kurring shows up on Claudia's doorstep because her neighbors called in a noise complaint because she was screaming at her dad because he molested her when she was a child. But out of that swirling miasma of sin and suffering—out of the everyday complications of life—comes the possibility for redemption.

Jim, who demonstrates throughout the film that he walks as a Christian should, in the footsteps of Jesus, has a surprise for Claudia. If to be a Christian is about showing radical love, then Claudia has accepted a date with someone who can accept her as she is and forgive her anything. The entire movie builds up to one moment: after listening to Jim gently but firmly tell her that he wants to be with her, that she is a good person, and that he will accept her, no matter what, Claudia turns to the camera, and in the last image of the film, she smiles.

It's a decision to accept grace, it follows from all that has come before, and although this decision is not the end but only a beginning, this smile shows us how God can bring life out of death, redemption out of suffering. Claudia and the other characters in *Magnolia* will bear scars from their experiences. But scars, the Rev. William Sloane Coffin wrote, "are wounds that have healed, not without a trace, but have healed nonetheless."[25] A world scarred with past pain is still a world led toward healing through the powerful grace and love of God.

Chapter Five

Peace and Justice
How Do We Live a Righteous Life?

Living a Life That Matters

One of my favorite films about redemption is *Groundhog Day*, a film in which obnoxious weatherman Phil Connor (Bill Murray) is stuck in the same day over and over again. Every morning he wakes up to "I Got You, Babe" on the clock radio in his room in the small town in rural Pennsylvania where he's been sent to cover Groundhog Day. An overbearing (say it with me), self-centered person who can't see past the end of his own needs, he first uses this strange chronal disjunction for his own satisfaction. In one day's cycle, for example, he learns how to meet and chat up Nancy (Marita Geraghty), so that the next day he can sleep with her. But mostly, he has his eyes on his producer, Rita (Andie MacDowell). She's smart and pretty and genuine and *good* and he falls for her— but no matter how hard he tries, how much information he gains about her, how much he learns in the march of days, she doesn't want to sleep with him. In a montage that indicates the passing of a vast number of Phil's days, Rita slaps him good night, in a number of locations, in a number of ways. Because, you see, ultimately even if he has managed to learn about French poetry and can give her favorite toast—"I like to drink to world peace"—to try to get under her skin, Rita doesn't like Phil because Phil is not a likable person.

One morning, watching him eat a table full of cholesterol-laden breakfast, drink coffee from the carafe, and smoke—since Phil doesn't have to worry about blood pressure, lung cancer, or love handles—she quotes a poem from Sir Walter Scott that begins, "The wretch, concentered all in self."

His inability to escape himself and his inability to make Rita fall for him drives him into despair. He kills himself, time and again—only to awake anew the next day, every next day.

At last, the patter of the disc jockeys on his clock radio as he awakens is a description of his life:

> *It's cold out there today.*
> *It's cold out there every day.*

"What would you do," he asks a drunk in a bowling alley, "if you were stuck in one place and every day was exactly the same, and nothing that you did mattered?"

Well, the drunk replies, that sounds like a pretty good description of my life.

Maybe it's because he's inspired by Rita's innate goodness: one night as he tells her all the things he admires about her, he says, "I've never seen anyone that's nicer to people than you are. And the first time I saw you, something happened to me."

Maybe it's because he grows to care about the homeless old street person who keeps on dying at the end of every one of his days. Maybe it's because he gets a good look at himself—but one day he tells Rita, "I *am* a jerk."

In any case, Phil stops amusing himself by sleeping with available women who aren't Rita, and robbing the armored car, and all of the other things he has done to amuse himself. He stops throwing himself off buildings and putting the bed-and-breakfast's toaster in his tub to escape his life. He stops trying to seduce Rita, which he finally realizes he can't accomplish in his current state. One night when he's gotten her into his room by being honest and genuine with her, he doesn't even try to kiss her.

And he begins living a life where even if every day is exactly the same, the things he does do matter.

The book of James is an important part of the Bible, because it corrects an impression that far too many people have about

Christian faith: that faith in Jesus is the only important thing in the Christian life. The Pauline letters, written in the midst of controversy about whether one had be Jewish and adhere to Jewish law to be saved, constantly tell us that faith in Christ crucified is the important thing, not adherence to laws or works. They were valuable words for Paul's audiences in their context, balanced halfway between the Jewish synagogues and the Roman world. But from the example of Christ, who healed the blind, the sick, the lame, and the insane, who fed the hungry, and who raised the dead, it seems clear that being Christlike requires more than simple belief.

James says it in this way:

> What good is it, my brothers and sisters, if you say you have faith but do not have works? Can faith save you? If a brother or sister is naked and lacks daily food, and one of you says to them, "Go in peace; keep warm and eat your fill," and yet you do not supply their bodily needs, what is the good of that? So faith by itself, if it has no works, is dead.
>
> But someone will say, "You have faith and I have works." Show me your faith apart from your works, and I by my works will show you my faith.[1]

At the end of *Groundhog Day*, Phil demonstrates his changed nature by what his typical day now looks like, a day that begins with a poetic weather broadcast accepting his fate and is filled with loving acts and good works. He is kind to his obnoxious insurance salesman friend from high school, catches ungrateful children falling out of trees, changes a flat tire for a carload of old women, saves the life of a man choking to death, gives marriage counseling to two kids who are getting hitched—and so on, and so forth. *Groundhog Day* is a funny and beautiful story about how we might live a Christlike life—a righteous life.

By helping others out of sincere regard for them, Phil not only finds joy, he also gets the girl. At the Groundhog Dance, Rita looks around at all the people who seem to think so much of Phil, all the people he's helped, and she realizes that he is not the person she thought he was. He has changed into something better, and his works demonstrate it.

Working for Justice

Movies are full of examples of heroes and heroines who have battled the odds, changed lives, saved the world, and these stories can be powerful examples for us about the life that comes after conversion. Remember when Jules Winnfield said he was going to wander the earth like Caine in *Kung Fu*, doing good? Well, that's a model of the redeemed life we're going to examine through the movies, and we're going to do it primarily by looking at the Christian imperatives for justice and peace. In recent years, many theologians, particularly those from two-thirds world countries (what we sometimes call third world, not recognizing that most of the world's people are, by our standards, "underdeveloped" and living in conditions of poverty), have called the church to a greater awareness of justice issues, and even to make the work of justice the primary mission of the church.

In his 1964 Nobel Peace Prize acceptance speech, like all of his public proclamations as much a sermon as a speech, Baptist minister Dr. Martin Luther King Jr. set out the challenge of Christian living in this way:

> I have the audacity to believe that peoples everywhere can have three meals a day for their bodies, education and culture for their minds, and dignity, equality, and freedom for their spirits. I believe that what self-centered men have torn down, other-centered men can build up. I still believe that one day mankind will bow before the altars of God and be crowned triumphant over war and bloodshed, and nonviolent redemptive good will proclaim the rule of the land.[2]

And where does the church fit into this peace and justice? Priest and theologian Gustavo Gutièrrez, in his seminal work *A Theology of Liberation*, argues that "by preaching the Gospel message, by its sacraments, and by the charity of its members, the church proclaims and shelters the gift of the Kingdom of God in the heart of human history. The Christian community professes a 'faith which works through charity.' It is—at least ought to be—real charity, action, and commitment to the service of men."[3]

In the work of Dorothy Day with the poor here in America and of Mother Teresa of Calcutta with the lepers and poor of her land, we can clearly see faith that works through charity—and a saintliness that should call all of us toward their examples. If there are two more perfect followers of Christ in the last century, I should be pleased to know of them.

Still, many American Christians are happy to rest on readings of the Pauline letters that suggest that faith and belief are the most important things for the Christian life today. They practice their faith on Sundays or in the privacy of their own homes. Perhaps they oppose some immoral practices or work toward laws banning strip clubs near elementary schools or selling alcohol on Sundays. But I want to suggest that this reading of Christianity ignores both biblical imperatives and changing notions about how religion should work in our changing world. Even many evangelical Christians today are convinced that to be Christian is to do God's work in the world, which we will know by what Jesus did—feed the hungry, alleviate suffering, promote peace.

How can we be sure that this is what Jesus would have us do? Besides the Gospel witness, there's the heritage within which he grew up. Christians forget Jesus' genealogy at their own peril. Jesus was a practicing Jew who taught and spoke primarily to his own people, and while he was like the prophets in proposing a new vision of what faith in God might look like, he did not propose turning our backs on the body of wisdom and revelation he had found formative. I have not come to destroy the law, Jesus said, but to fulfill it.[4] The Greek verb that we translate "fulfill" is πληρῶσαι (*plerosai*), and what it means is to show the true meaning or full significance. Jesus is saying that in him and his works the Hebrew law is finding complete expression, which is about as far as you can get from saying it's not important.

So what does the law say? The Hebrew Bible expresses twin concerns. The greatest, of course, is found in the First Commandment and Deuteronomy 6:4, in the prayer now called the Shema and prayed to this day by Jews in the morning and the evening: "Hear, Israel, the Lord is our God, the Lord is One."

So one primary concern is that the one true God should be recognized and worshiped.

The other primary concern is for justice.
God was considered to be the ultimate source of justice for the
nations and for individuals. As Temba L. J. Mafico notes of the
Hebrew Bible, "God is portrayed as having a special concern for
the poor, particularly the widow, the fatherless, and the oppressed."[5]
A special compassion for the widow, for the orphan, and for the
resident alien is mandated in many passages in the Old Testament, and in Deuteronomy, it could not be put more bluntly:
"Cursed be anyone who deprives the alien, the orphan, and the
widow of justice."[6]

The Christian Testament too is filled with examples of concern
for the poor, the sick, and those who fell through society's cracks.
After Mary of Nazareth, a poor peasant girl, receives the news that
she is to bring the Son of God into the world, she sings a song we
today call the Magnificat, which celebrates God's preferential concern for the oppressed:

> He has brought down the powerful from their thrones,
>   and lifted up the lowly;
> he has filled the hungry with good things,
>   and sent the rich away empty.[7]

Jesus too seems drawn to those who struggle for their daily
bread, and why should this surprise us? Our depictions of the
imperial Christ ruling from heaven have made us forget that the
earthly Jesus was one of those who struggled. John Dominic
Crossan tells us that if Jesus was indeed from a family of carpen-
ters (or handymen; either translation is likely) in first-century
Galilee, he would have been reckoned "lower than the peasants in
social class," and have been right on the cusp of being one of those
in the economic abyss: beggars, day laborers, bandits, or slaves.[8]
In the Gospel stories about Jesus' life, we can see that he loved and
cared for the poor and weak, particularly in the Gospel of Mark
where he healed, ate with, and interacted with one after another of
society's downtrodden, exiled, or oppressed. In doing so, he often
brought opprobrium upon himself, paying dearly in the currency
of the first century, honor and shame. His opponents took Jesus to
task for eating with sinners, gathering food on the Sabbath, even

for healing on the Sabbath. But Jesus told them that the Sabbath was made for human beings, not vice versa, and he asked them, "Is it lawful to do good or to do harm on the sabbath, to save life or to kill?"[9]

In other words, is it more important to be pious?

Or to be righteous?

Warden Norton (Bob Gunton) in *The Shawshank Redemption* tells incoming prisoners, "I believe in two things: discipline and the Bible. Here you'll receive both." The warden may believe in the Bible, but he's still an example of far too many pious Christians portrayed in American films who profess belief but don't display it in their daily lives, while his "discipline" is a powerful example of injustice. What we believe may be important, but simply calling yourself a believer of Jesus doesn't make you one. In *Batman Begins*, Batman (Christian Bale) says, "It's not who I am, but what I do that defines me." Batman puts his actions where his words are, and that is in the quest to make the world a better place for the oppressed and those who need justice.

So did Jesus.

If Jesus were around today, I think he'd be a powerful proponent of the Jewish concept of "tikkun olam," the idea that we are called to work toward the healing of the world. In his constant references to God's kingdom, that's what he seems to have been talking about: a world without war, a world in which justice reigns, a world in which the poor and the oppressed are treated with dignity and their needs are met. Jesus actually inaugurates his ministry in the Gospel of Luke by reading from the scroll of Isaiah and proclaiming that all of these words are coming true now: "The Spirit of the Lord is upon me, because he has anointed me to bring good news to the poor. He has sent me to proclaim release to the captives and recovery of sight to the blind, to let the oppressed go free, to proclaim the year of the Lord's favor."[10]

Justice, then, is one of the most basic of Christian tenets, and this belief that the oppressed are privileged in the eyes of God is paralleled by the special concern for justice we can find in many films. In the films of the Depression, we can find movies wrestling with the problem of economic justice; throughout its history, Hollywood has released powerful and sometimes prophetic films about prejudice; and although dramatic violence has always been a mainstay of American films, we can also find an awareness that violence is destructive of everything we hold sacred, and that there can be no real justice without peace.

Economic Justice and the Films of the Great Depression

During the Great Depression, studios began making a genre of comedies called screwball comedies that featured the eccentric rich, often thrown into contact with people of the lower classes, as we saw in *The Philadelphia Story*. Sometimes, as in *It Happened One Night*, *The Lady Eve*, and *My Man Godfrey*, love crossed the social barriers, and—at least dramatically—leveled classes. These films do, in some ways, sugarcoat disparity in a time of national economic upheaval by showing how members of the poor or working classes might "marry up," and how the upper classes seemingly consisted mostly of wacky, zany, lovable people. But all the same, their portrayal of different classes was a rare thing in American culture.

We like to believe that we Americans live in a classless society; the mere act of suggesting that this is untrue or pointing out the disparity between rich and poor can open one to the charge of conducting "class warfare." But as Gutièrrez notes, whenever we deny that there is economic disparity or refuse to discuss it, we automatically weigh in on the side of the status quo, a status quo in which many are poor but only a very few are wealthy.[11]

It Happened One Night is not as socially aware as later films by director Frank Capra like *Mr. Smith Goes to Washington*, *Mr. Deeds Goes to Town*, or even *It's a Wonderful Life*, but it does focus on the class distinctions between spoiled heiress Ellie Andrews (Claudette Colbert) and out-of-work reporter Peter Warne (Clark Gable). Gable teaches Ellie how the little people live as they travel across country, and moreover, the movie emphasizes that whether a man has money or not is a measure of his character. As we saw in the discussion of class and prejudice in *The Philadelphia Story*, characters can agree that some poor people are princes, and some princes are clods. But does anything change with that recognition? No. The rich guy may be a clod, but at least he's a rich clod.

My Man Godfrey manages to express criticism of the moneyed classes (what the movie characterizes as the idle rich) while remaining socially conservative; homeless butler Godfrey (William Powell) does end up marrying rich Miss Irene Bullock (Claudette Colbert)—but he actually comes from the upper classes himself. It turns out that he's just living at the city dump because he's been in the dumps about being dumped. And at the end, it turns out she's lost all her money so she's not rich any more. But he's saved her fortune—

I know, it's confusing. All these screwball comedies are like this, a mile a minute and often puzzling even if you've paid close attention. But what's important is that however things end up, this movie does make some important points about the necessity for justice.

The movie begins with rich socialites scouring the dump for the "forgotten men" they need for a scavenger hunt. Irene's sister Cornelia (Gail Patrick) offers Godfrey five dollars to be her forgotten man; he tells her off, but takes a liking to Irene and agrees to go back to the Waldorf-Ritz Hotel to help her win. After Godfrey is pronounced an authentic bum, he turns and rails on the idle rich for their antics. Even though the criticism is tempered somewhat by our later discovery that Godfrey is from an "old family," one of the class he's criticizing, this is still radical for its time—and perhaps, for ours. What the idle rich should be doing is revealed at the end of the movie, when we discover that Godfrey has built a nightclub to feed and house people during the winter, and to give them jobs during the summer. (Perhaps the idle rich would be okay, the movie thus suggests, if they were just a little more active.)

Godfrey has said that "the only difference between a derelict and a man is a job," and in this concern for people's everyday needs, we see an idea that the church must explore. Dr. Martin Luther King said that the gospel was concerned with the whole person, with the body as well as the soul, "not only his spiritual well-being but also his material well-being," and he often said that any church that didn't take this into consideration would become an irrelevant social club—a building full of idle Christians, perhaps.[12]

One of my favorite films from the Depression era is *The Adventures of Robin Hood*, which features Errol Flynn at his swashbuckling best. (Whatever that means; I myself have never buckled a swash.)

You all know the Robin Hood story, but perhaps you haven't considered how radical the story actually is, the contempt it reflects for governments that don't care for all of their people, and the practical and even religious elements that appear in it. First, the land has fallen into disrepair because the King of England has gotten his religious priorities screwed up. He's left the country to follow a call to the Crusades, a siren call about saving his own soul through pious military action, and he's left his rat-fink brother Prince John (Claude Rains) in charge. John is not burdened by religious sentiments of any kind; he just wants to squeeze the people for all they've got. And all the structures of English society—the nobility, the church—have fallen in alongside him.

But one man—Robin of Locksley—rises up to help the oppressed. He stands up for a hunter who has killed the king's deer. The penalty is death—apparently it is better for the poor to starve than for the aristocracy to be deprived of their amusement—but Robin saves him. When it becomes clear that he cannot make his voice heard through the normal structures of his society—Prince John tries to have him killed at a state dinner, and on sundry other occasions—Robin sets himself in opposition to his society, gathers a group of disciples willing to follow him in his radical mission, and makes them take an oath to despoil the rich and give to the poor, to shelter the old and the helpless, and to protect women. All of the things that his society refuses to do for the oppressed, Robin accepts as his personal mission.

In chapter 2 we saw how some of our dramatic analogues for Christ were countercultural antiheroes, and Robin Hood too seems to fit this mold; in many ways, he stands as a figure of Christ. That idea may be disturbing for you, and my intent is certainly not to be sacrilegious. Yet who would we say is being more Christlike, an outlaw who steals from the wealthy to preserve the lives of the poor and weak, or a pious priest of the church who collects alms from them but refuses to be their advocate in front of Prince John?

I'd throw my money behind the outlaw preaching the counter-cultural, and I probably wouldn't be the lone bettor. Richard Horsley argues that Jesus' whole mission was to preach "that God was bringing an end to the demonic and political powers dominating his society so that a renewal of individual and social life would be possible."[13]

If you'd given Jesus a bow and arrow, I wonder if he would have looked at all like Errol Flynn?

Maid Marian (Olivia de Haviland) is slowly converted to Robin's point of view, although at first she cares more about his manners: He's brusque and he breaks the rules. But gradually she becomes intrigued as she sees his selflessness, the people he has helped. What sort of man risks his life to fight injustice? she wonders, and she asks him flat out, "What's your reward?"

Later Marian herself stands up against King John and his nobles like the convert she has become. She, at least, is sold on Robin's message of radical redistribution of wealth to save the least of these, and like the saints of the early church, she is willing to suffer punishment and imprisonment for following Robin.

It's great that Robin is willing to risk his life to help the poor, widow, and orphan, and it makes for a wonderful story. But what does it mean that the man who wants to bring economic justice to England is an outlaw and a vigilante? It means that English society is not doing the work that it is called to do, the protection and welfare of all its citizens, rich and poor. It means that the society has set the rules so that the rich get richer, and the poor lose what little they have. And it reminds me of the story of Jesus in more than just recounting how a redeemer gathered a group of apostles around him.

Jesus lived in a society with great disparity between rich and poor, as did Robin and his Merry Men, as do we. (Is it class warfare to point out that in the year 2000 the three biggest shareholders in Microsoft controlled more wealth than all 600 million Africans combined, or that the three richest people in the world have accumulated more wealth than the combined gross domestic product of the forty-eight poorest countries?)[14] The poor in Jesus' time were harried in much the same way that the poor of Merry Olde England suffered, and the religious leaders of either time were no help—they were sometimes even a hindrance. Over and over again, Jesus came into conflict with his opponents, the Pharisees, scribes, and Temple leaders (who are sometimes generically called "Jews," although of course virtually all of the characters in the Gospel narratives, including Jesus, are Jewish). Often their conflict arose because, although both may have read the Scriptures seriously and prayerfully, they read the same Bible in radically different ways.

Jesus interpreted the Holy Scriptures, the Torah, through the examples of the prophets, a reading that called for justice for the poor and oppressed. Jesus' opponents chose to read the Torah "through a priestly filter concerned with purity codes," making their religion more about individual connection to God than it was about helping people in need.[15]

Matthew 23 shows an example. In a long section during which he confronted his opponents, Jesus said, "Woe to you, scribes and Pharisees, hypocrites! For you tithe mint, dill, and cummin [spices not even legislated in the Law], and have neglected the weightier matters of the law: justice and mercy and faith. It is these you ought to have practiced without neglecting the others. You blind guides! You strain out a gnat but swallow a camel!

"Woe to you, scribes and Pharisees, hypocrites! For you clean the outside of the cup and of the plate, but inside they are full of greed and self-indulgence."[16]

Jesus stood up against the powers that be to preach and act out how true faith should be about generosity and self-sacrifice. At the coronation of Prince John, Robin and his men, dressed in the religious robes of friars, rise up and resist the installation of a ruler who cares so little about the littlest. Many scholars suggest that Jesus' message too was a political (as well as a religious) one against a repressive system; he too was a disturber of the imperial peace, and he did, after all, die a political death, crucifixion, at the hands of the Roman occupation government.

Both the Robin Hood and Gospel stories thus feature counter-cultural heroes working against a corrupt and corrupting system to try to bring justice. We might ask, what is the responsibility of a society to its least privileged? Sure, King John was a creep, but Robin Hood was wrong for breaking the law. Can't we rely on charity, on the work of churches, or on the "rising tide raises all boats" philosophy that says when the rich are happy, everyone in a society will eventually benefit?

My friend Roy Herron, a lawyer, legislator, and former minister, is a good resource for questions like these. Roy writes that "the Bible calls us to shape our society in such a way that the poor are provided for and justice is ensured. This is to be a matter of basic political and social structure, not something left to individual charity and to chance."[17]

And when our society fails, even if our society has built that failure into laws and policies, then we have a responsibility to stand for what is right. Aquinas would tell you that if a law doesn't comport with natural law—and what law enshrining injustice would?—then it should and must be changed.

We can see our failure to pursue this biblical mandate for social justice in films like John Ford's adaptation of John Steinbeck's *The Grapes of Wrath*. This story about the great exodus of farmers and workers from the Dust Bowl to the West Coast was one of Hollywood's most powerful visions of the lives of the poor and oppressed. Unlike the poor and working-class characters in the screwball comedies, the lives of the destitute Tom Joad (Henry Fonda) and his family don't seem quaint or filled with simple pleasures, and none of them meet, let alone marry, any of the wealthy. No, the Joads' slow exodus from dying Oklahoma to California is no pleasure cruise; people take advantage of them instead of helping them; the family matriarch dies during the crossing of the desert. And even when they reach the promised land, California, they find that it's not a land of milk and honey. Here, too, they are cheated, treated like animals, and Tom ends up having to run for his life after killing a man. It's a sad story that, under our very noses, still takes place today. When Jesus said that we would always have the poor with us, this wasn't because he thought that this was a good thing, and it wasn't intended to keep us from helping them; it was because he knew that people would always be drawn to wealth and power, and the surest way to them is over the backs of others.

The Grapes of Wrath is a powerful indictment of a society that didn't take seriously the moral mandate to take care of its people, and in the Okies' flight from their homes and all that they know and love, I can't help but think of recent events. Who didn't feel shame at the sight of poor black New Orleanians herded like cattle into the Superdome—or floating as corpses in toxic flood waters in their old neighborhoods after Hurricane Katrina devastated the Gulf Coast?

Those New Orleanians with money and cars were frightened but fine. Those who just had cars were frightened and not fine; if I'd been forced to leave my home and run for my life, my own resources would have run out pretty quickly, although at least I could have gotten out of the state.

And those with no money and no cars stayed, and suffered, and some of them died.

So *The Grapes of Wrath* isn't simply a history lesson about a horrible time in America's past. It's a reminder that when we allow some people to die or suffer because they're poor, we are failing the most basic tests of morality presented to us by our beliefs. *The Grapes of Wrath* shows us that poverty robs people of dignity, makes them afraid, and steals from them the God-given shape of what they might do and be—and that is simply wrong.

Today, we live in a nation in which over 40 million people lack health insurance. Let me say that slowly: over 40 million people in America—including some people I know and love—do not have insurance that would allow them to get the regular health care they need or the medications they require to live well or even to live, period. We live in a nation in which our accumulated individual debt far outweighs the money we've managed to save. We live in a nation in which some of the working poor take on two and three jobs to try to keep a roof over their family's heads and some sort of food on the table and a nation where some American politicians argue that we should cut taxes on those whose money does all the work for them, even to the extent of not taxing the estates of the wealthiest after they have passed away and no longer have any excuse to keep it.

So the lessons we can learn from the films of the past are not simply historical—economic injustice continues today, and more recent films (including *The Apartment, Norma Rae,* and *Syriana*) talk about the exploitation of those who have less by those who have more—yet who want more, still.

Prejudice and Equality

Justice is about more than simply economic justice. Justice is also about sexual equality, that is, treating men and women with equal respect—and about how we treat those who differ from us—those who are alien, those who have a different color skin, those who believe or live or love differently than we do. We can find numerous Old Testament injunctions to treat the resident alien with respect and justice, many of them remembering that, over and over again, the children of God had been exiles in a strange land. In his parable about the Good Samaritan, Jesus said that we were to love not just those who were like us, but all people, even those who were our enemies. The Samaritan in Jesus' story treated the wounded man by the side of the road not as a hated Jew but as a precious fellow human.

Again, Hollywood can give us some pointers to help us seek justice in our relations with others. First, Hollywood films have long found the issue of female equality to be a rich mine for dramatic stories. *Alice Doesn't Live Here Anymore, Silkwood, The Color Purple, Howard's End,* and *Erin Brockovich* are films that have featured strong women standing up for themselves, and they only scratch the surface.

Katherine Hepburn (as we saw in *The Philadelphia Story*) made her name playing strong-willed independent women (and being one, off the screen). In the films she made with Spencer Tracy, the competence of women was often a major theme. *Adam's Rib,* which pitted Hepburn and Tracy against each other in court, actually centered on the question of whether women were as competent as men. Another of Hepburn's films, *The African Queen*, had her portraying Rose Sayer, a spinster missionary in Africa during World War I who succeeds in talking a reluctant riverboat captain, Charlie Allnut (Humphrey Bogart, of course), into going down the river and attacking a German gunboat. Her courage and determination through a trying and dangerous journey downstream are apparent, both to us, and to the initially skeptical Charlie Allnut, who is at last so taken with Rose's pluck and tenacity that he asks her to marry him.

Sexual prejudice also carries over to personal sexuality; we have been hard-pressed to accept as equal people who love in ways different from the heterosexual norm. In recent years, a number of important Hollywood films have examined prejudice against gays, lesbians, transgendered persons, and others who have sometimes been considered sexual outcasts. Tom Hanks won his first Academy Award in 1993 for his portrayal of Andrew Beckett, a gay man dying of AIDS in *Philadelphia*. Hilary Swank won her first Academy Award for her portrayal of a transgendered teen, Brandon Teena, in 1999's *Boys Don't Cry*.

Both of these movies are, in a sense, "issue" movies about prejudice. In *Philadelphia*, Andrew Beckett is the main character, but he's a static character. The character who has the most dynamic story line in the movie is Beckett's homophobic attorney, Joe Miller (Denzel Washington), who moves from statements like "Some of these people make me sick" to "This is the essence of discrimination: formulating opinions about others not based on their individual merits, but rather on their membership in a group with assumed characteristics."

Brokeback Mountain, however, is a movie that was seen both by people who championed gay rights and by some who just wanted to go to a movie on Saturday night, and it swept the country in 2005. Whether you had seen it or not, you knew about it, and often the fact that it was a gay love story was no more important than the fact that it was a powerful human love story.

Many Christians, of course, consider homosexuality to be sinful, and American denominations including the Presbyterian and Episcopal Churches have faced recent divisions over the place of gay men and women in the church. But ultimately justice is not about whether you think someone deserves it or not. The Good Samaritan story doesn't offer us any outs where prejudice is concerned; it never says that the Samaritan liked the wounded man. It doesn't say that he changed his mind about Jewish religious practice or politics. It doesn't say that he approved of him.

It simply says that the Samaritan treated him as a fellow child of God and gave him life when others left him there to die.

What makes *Brokeback Mountain* so important is not that it contains homosexual characters; it's that unlike *Philadelphia*, for example, which, for all its strengths, treats Beckett more as a representative than as a human being, the characters in *Brokeback Mountain* are human beings who happen to be gay. They have strengths and weaknesses, they sin and they suffer, and, like all people, their lives would be immeasurably better if people could understand them and treat them with dignity and respect.

Racial prejudice has been perhaps the longest lasting and most challenging issue of American history, and Hollywood has often been on target with films about intolerance and justice that can remind us that loving selectively is not an option for Christians. Some films, like *Crossfire* and *Gentleman's Agreement*, addressed prejudice from the standpoint of American anti-Semitism, while others have looked at the treatment of people based on skin color, as in *Pinky*. But two films have confronted not just racial prejudice, but the act of prejudice itself, and we'll close our discussion of American prejudice with analyses of two monumental films, one made by a black American director, Spike Lee—*Do the Right Thing*—and one made by a white Canadian director, Paul Haggis—*Crash*.

Spike Lee's films have almost always concentrated on issues of race and society. He made a biographical film about the black leader Malcolm X, a moving documentary about the children killed in the bombing of the 16th Street Baptist Church in 1963, and *Clockers,* about crime in an impoverished black neighborhood. *Do the Right Thing*, still regarded by many critics as Lee's greatest film, is a multifaceted look at the problem of prejudice as it walks the streets of Brooklyn on a hot summer day.

In this film, Lee plays Mookie, a pizza deliveryman for the neighborhood pizza joint—which happens to be owned by Sal (Danny Aiello), an Italian American. Except for the pizza place and the corner store, which is run by a Korean family, the neighborhood is almost exclusively populated by African Americans, and on this, the hottest day of the summer, racial tensions rise when Buggin Out (Giancarlo Esposito) decides that the people of the neighborhood should boycott Sal's Famous until he puts some pictures of African Americans on the wall of his restaurant next to all the Italian Americans.

Prejudice is a strange thing. Sal's oldest son Vito (Richard Edson) is a virulent racist who can't stand coming into the neighborhood: "I detest this place like a sickness." He hectors Mookie, calling him lazy—which he is—and spreading his prejudice everywhere. His younger brother, Pino (John Turturro) considers Mookie a friend and is more open. And Sal? Sal is proud of who he is, proud of where he came from—and proud of his place in the community. He's been there for years, and it gives him a good feeling knowing that many of the kids walking those streets have been raised on and nourished by his pizza.

Racism is a complex problem that boils down to perception. Do we see the Other as human and worthy of our respect and God's love? Some of the characters in *Do the Right Thing* are selectively prejudiced: they hate blacks, let's say, but love Michael Jordan and Michael Jackson, arguing that they're "not black." Others hate everyone on the other side of the divide, without complication.

One of the most famous sequences in the movie is one in which members of different ethnic groups talk about another group that offends them, calling them horrible names—and then giving way to a member of that group who looks into the camera, opens his mouth—and starts telling you about an ethnic group that *he* can't stand. It's stunning: many of us have gotten so used to living politely with racism that we never hear these virulent names spoken, although the structures that segregate us still exist, and much of the bad feeling as well.

Do the Right Thing ends with a violent confrontation in which the racism on both sides comes to a tragic end and the neighborhood is left to pick up the pieces. Earlier in the movie, the mayor, the neighborhood drunk and sage played by actor and civil rights activist Ossie Davis, gives Mookie some advice: "Always do the right thing."

But what is the right thing? Mookie does do something: during the middle of a violent stand-off between the police and people in the neigborhood, he throws a trash can through Sal's plate glass window—and into his place of employment—and redirects the anger and violence toward the pizza parlor. Buildings are less important than people. But that is hard for Sal to understand the next morning as he sits in the ashes of his business.

Crash, which won Best Picture at the 2006 Academy Awards, is another of the most powerful films on prejudice ever to come out of Hollywood. During the course of its two hours, it does repeatedly what *Do the Right Thing* does in that section where the bigots turn to the camera—it pushes the fact of prejudice directly in front of us and shoves our noses in it. Cowriter and director Paul Haggis and his writing partner Bobby Maresco decided that if they were going to make a movie about prejudice, they had to show intolerance in all its ugliness, and although they constantly asked each other during the writing of the script if they could get away with such horrifying bluntness, the first half of *Crash* startles and offends mightily but has the unmistakable ring of truth. The truth can scar, but it also can set us free, and that seems to be its function in this film.

Race is, as we have said, the central problem of our American lives. Jim Wallis has called it "America's original sin, and it resonates with people of every tradition and every background, with people of color who feel they've been marginalized and with people of Anglo descent who fear the coming of change they can't control."[18] By employing racial prejudice as its central organizing factor, *Crash* shows us a world in which everyone has a bias of some sort, bias that seems to emerge spontaneously in the emotionally charged collisions of our day-to-day lives. But the movie does more than simply note the problem and move on. Like *Do the Right Thing*, by showing us people wrestling with this central problem and resolving that they want to do better, want to *be* better, *Crash* proves to be a deeply ethical and spiritual film.

What makes *Crash* even more involving is how, as in the films of Alfred Hitchcock, we find that we are doing more than just watching a movie; we are actually being implicated in the prejudice it relates. Steve Davis notes that the movie "invites you to make comfortable judgments about its myriad characters based on [your] first impressions and to pigeonhole them in uncomplicated, black-and-white terms."[19] In other words, the first appearances of characters in the film invite us to establish our own prejudices about them.

But as is often true when we sink to prejudice, we discover that our first opinions about these characters are not sufficient; they're more complex people than we first thought, and they surprise us. The two articulate young African Americans arguing about why people stereotype them as violent, for example, turn out to actually be carjackers; the Mexican American locksmith accused of being a gangbanger turns out to be a loving father who works multiple shifts to pull his family out of a dangerous neighborhood; the Persian storeowner who seems to be victimized by others almost commits the most horrific violence in the film.

Virtually every character in *Crash* displays appalling prejudice at some point during the film. And most also display bravery, compassion, and wisdom.

I thought the most powerful story line—and perhaps the most redemptive—concerned the almost-fatal intersection of racist cop Officer Ryan (Matt Dillon) and Officer Hanson (Ryan Phillipe) pulling over the SUV containing a black driver, Cameron (Terrence Howard), and his wife, Christine (Thandie Newton), a light-skinned African American. Ryan forces Cameron to perform a sobriety test, and then orders both passengers out and against the side of the vehicle, where he proceeds to sexually assault Christine, under the guise of searching her for weapons. It is a humiliating violation for her and horrifying for Cameron, but she is outraged that her husband pleads for their release instead of physically intervening to stop it. Meanwhile Officer Hanson stands to the side, appalled at what is happening, but silent.

This scene by itself is so rich that it deserves close attention. First, how many times have we stood by, silent, when we should have acted? During his imprisonment in Birmingham, Dr. King wrote, "We will have to repent in this generation not merely for the vitriolic words and actions of the bad people, but for the appalling silence of the good people. We must see that human progress never rolls in on wheels of inevitability. It comes through the tireless efforts and persistent work of men willing to be co-workers with God."[20]

Hanson could have said something; to his credit, he later tries to report Ryan, and does transfer to another assignment. But during that moment when it would really have meant something: appalling silence.

Rape and sexual violation are rarely sexual crimes; they typically grow out of anger, hatred, and the desire to humiliate and hurt. Before he and his partner clocked in, Officer Ryan had been trying to get some help from an African American administrator at his father's HMO about his father's treatment. His father is in agony, something hasn't been diagnosed right, yet no one will listen. That, unfortunately, includes Shaniqua (Loretta Devine); their conversation at last degenerates into racial insult, and Ryan is left furious and with no solution for his father. So his desire to humiliate the black couple—and especially this mouthy black woman—grows out of his own recent experience.

It's part of *Crash*'s strategy to show that people are always more complicated than the one-line stereotypes we might try to pin onto them. While his treatment of Cameron and Christine is inexcusable, Officer Ryan's character is not so easy to pigeonhole as it first appears. *New Yorker* film critic David Denby notes of this scene, "as we later find out, a racist can also be a good son and a good cop."[21] This is the startling and hopeful power of *Crash*; people behave at their worst and people behave at their best, and it becomes abundantly clear by watching them which it is we should be doing.

One of the most painful scenes in a film full of challenging situations comes when Cameron and Christine arrive home after the traffic stop. She berates him for not standing up for her, for not intervening physically as she was sexually violated. It is an argument that, tragically, goes back in this country hundreds of years to the time of slavery when black men could not protect their women. Cameron argues that Officer Ryan and his partner had guns, that he had no real choice, this is L.A., after all, the Los Angeles Police Department of Rodney King fame, but his arguments are unsatisfying even to him.

His wife was sexually violated before his very eyes.

A real man would have done something.

But what? What kind of society presents any of its members with such a choice: get yourself killed or seethe silently at injustice because you are afraid that speaking out or protecting someone you love will cost you your life?

Officer Hanson and Cameron cross paths again; when a string of events leads the police to pull Cameron over, he gets out of the SUV determined to prove his manhood by suicidally defying them, and Hanson comes in between Cameron and their raised guns and talks both sides into sense. It may be an attempt to make up for his inaction the night before, but it is still an act of real bravery. Without his intervention, Cameron would probably have been shot dead, his bravery at last proven to Christine, maybe, but his life extinguished.

Officer Ryan and Christine meet again as well. In what has become the signature scene of the film, Ryan runs headlong up a hill to rescue a motorist stranded in an overturned SUV. He gets there, sees a woman inside (Christine, although Ryan doesn't know that), sees the gasoline dripping steadily from the tank, but despite the looming danger—the car that hit hers is on fire and the flames could ignite the gas from her tank—he crawls in to try to pull her loose.

It's already a dramatic reversal; we had thought this guy couldn't be lower, and here he is, putting his life on the line. But then, as they come face to face, they recognize each other, and it's hard to say who is more painfully stricken. Ryan is looking at the reminder of a degrading act he committed and now cannot put away from him; Christine is looking at an officer of the law who violated her body and her dignity, who drove a wedge between her and her husband. She screams at him not to touch her; it's clear at that moment that she would rather die than be rescued by him. Hasn't he already done enough to her?

Maybe Ryan sees that she'd rather die than be touched by him again; maybe down deep he isn't such a bad guy after all; or maybe something happens to him, something like that transformation we've been calling redemption, that makes him want to be a better person. Ryan has just told his former partner Officer Hanson, "Wait till you've been on the job a few more years. . . .Wait till you've been doing it a little longer. You think you know who you are? You have no idea." Sage advice from the jaded but streetwise cop to the idealistic rookie.

But now, confronted with the horrible reality of a human being in danger—and a human being he has wronged—Officer Ryan steps up to the challenge. He could leave her to burn; his sin would disappear with her. But maybe he is discovering who he is too.

As Christine screams at him to get away, he tries to calm her, until at last he shouts over her screaming that he's not going to hurt her. "I'm not going to touch you," he tells her. "But there's nobody else here yet, and that's gasoline there. We've got to get you out of here."

Gently—with surprising and genuine respect—he asks if he can reach across her lap to try and undo the seat belt. He pulls her dress down to cover her exposed thigh. And when she asks if he's going to get her out, he vows to her that he will.

The belt is stuck. The car down the hill ignites the pool of gasoline, and the SUV catches on fire, but still Ryan doesn't abandon Christine. When his partner and a bystander pull him out of the car to try to save his life, Ryan goes back into the burning SUV and pulls her free just before the tank blows.

As she's taken away, she turns back for a moment to look at him and shakes her head. Is he the man who molested her, or the man who saved her? How could either one share a body with the other?

And as the camera holds on Ryan, we imagine that he's probably thinking the same thing. From hatred and humiliation to recognition and rescue—all in the course of twenty-four hours.

At first glance it might seem that everyone in the movie is guilty of bigotry at some point, but if we look closely we'll see that the movie does have a moral center, the locksmith Daniel Ruiz (Michael Peña). Dissed as a gangbanger by a wealthy white house-wife (Sandra Bullock) who looks only at his tattoos, brown skin, and baggy pants, and as a thief by the Persian shopkeeper (Shaun Toub), Daniel never returns evil for evil. In one of the most beau-tiful scenes of the film, Daniel talks to his daughter about her fears of violence—they once lived in a neighborhood where a bullet went through her window, and he finds her sleeping on the floor, under her bed—and he tells her that he has an invisible magic cloak he has been meaning to give her, a Cloak of Impenetrability that will stop any bullet. At this moment, we aren't watching a brown person; we aren't watching a Hispanic. We're watching a father comforting his daughter, and the message, clearly, is that we are all alike underneath the skin.

It's a message we find in the Pauline Epistles, which talk over and over again about reconciling Jew and Gentile, master and slave, and it was one of the most remarkable things about the early Christian church. In a sermon he delivered in South Africa during apartheid, Archbishop Desmond Tutu pointed out how the Greco-Roman world segregated people by whether they were slave or free, rich or poor, man or woman. But in the early Christian church, "the world saw a veritable miracle unfolding before its very eyes as all sorts and conditions of women and men, rich and poor, slave and free, Jew and Gentile—all these came to belong in one fel-lowship, one *koinonia*, one communion. They did not regard each other just as equals . . . but as sisters and brothers, members of one family, God's family."[22]

In 1 John, we find

> Anyone who claims to be in the light but who hates brother and sister remains in the darkness still. Anyone who loves brother and sister abides in the light, and in the light there is no reason to stumble. But anyone who hates brother and sister remains in darkness and walks in darkness, without direction, blinded by the darkness.[23]

Some of the characters in *Crash* end up walking in darkness; redemption is offered, but not everyone accepts it. However, a surprising number of them are walking in the light, or at least headed toward it. Not that prejudice is cured (is it ever?), but these characters have seen that the world is—that people are—more complicated than prejudice allows for, and we have learned what it is we should do, both from what we've seen and how we've reacted to it.

Peace and Nonviolence

So why do we hate anyone? And why do we kill people we hate?

The problem of peace and nonviolent solutions to hatred and conflict are a particular challenge both for me (I love Hong Kong action movies and war films of every kind, from *Master and Commander* to *Star Wars*) and for our culture (our culture is violent, our popular culture is violent, and we have made violence such a default setting that to talk of peace today is synonymous with weakness or naiveté in the minds of some people). But the movies can give us valuable lessons on the important of peace, one of the primary callings of every Christian, both in what films say about violence and in what they don't.

It's a paradox. Some of the most exciting moments in film history do revolve around violent action. There's Dirty Harry: "Go ahead. Make my day." And the Terminator: "I'll be back." Sergeant York and John Wayne. Neo and Agent Smith. Even Yoda, that wizened little Jedi master who can do back flips while he swings a lightsaber. We find violence in so many films because it is dramatic conflict come to life—when people raise their fists or take up arms against each other, the battle for good and evil is joined tangibly and visibly.

But everyone also acknowledges these real-world truths: War is hell.

And violence shatters lives.

If we seek justice, then peace has to be a part of that seeking, because even more than deprivation, even more than prejudice, violence is the ultimate thief of life and happiness, and peace stands at the center of our Judeo-Christian understanding, "the hallmark of Christian life," according to Stanley Hauerwas.[24] In the Hebrew testament we hear that God orders Moses to bless the children of Israel with a particular blessing: "The LORD spoke to Moses, saying: The LORD bless you and keep you; the LORD make his face to shine upon you, and be gracious to you; the LORD lift up his countenance upon you, and give you peace."[25]

Jesus blesses his disciples similarly, so that the *Book of Common Prayer* reads, "Lord Jesus Christ, you said to your apostles, 'Peace I give you; my own peace I leave with you:' . . . give to us the peace and unity of that heavenly city where with the Father and Holy Spirit you live and reign, now and forever. AMEN."[26]

Peace is a gift of God. But in this broken world, we often choose violence instead, perhaps because we don't recall what violence really is and does, perhaps because it seems to be an easier solution.

Let's look, though, at one cinematic act of violence. It happens offstage. We don't see it, we don't hear it.

And yet clearly, this one instance of violence is a monumental act of injustice that affects not only its victim but others, just as a rock thrown into water sends concentric circles outward from its landing spot.

In *The Accidental Tourist*, director Lawrence Kasdan's adaptation of the Anne Tyler novel, the initiating action is something we only hear about, only see through the impact it has on those left behind. One night a boy named Ethan sneaks out of summer camp with a couple of his friends so that they can go get a burger. While they're in the restaurant, robbers come in, and before they leave, they shoot everyone inside.

After the event, Ethan's father and mother, Macon and Sarah (William Hurt and Kathleen Turner) collapse into their own griefs and their marriage breaks up. Macon becomes despondent, locked in mindless routine. Sarah tells him that she feels as if Ethan's murderer has killed her too. The world, she says, is evil. It has to be, for something like this to happen to an innocent boy.

Although *The Accidental Tourist* ends hopefully, at least for Macon, who finds a woman who can draw him out of his sadness and help him redeem the loss of his son, this single act of violence tells us a great deal. When we watch violence on the screen, we rarely have to imagine the aftereffects, which concern not only those who are killed or wounded, but all those who love them, depend on them, or know them.

As I write these words, America is at war with Muslim revolutionaries in Iraq, and our government is considering starting another war in the Middle East. (I pray that when you read this, both will be a distant memory.) I opposed the war in Iraq vocally and publicly, and was told that to do so was un-American and was giving comfort to the enemy (at that time, Saddam Hussein). I think of myself first as a Christian, then as a good and loyal American (we'll talk more about America and the church in our final chapter), and my protest was drawn from the ideals of Christian pacifism, the idea that we are to be like Christ, who forbade violence even against those who had come to arrest and take him to his show trial: "Suddenly, one of those with Jesus put his hand on his sword, drew it, and struck the slave of the high priest, cutting off his ear. Then Jesus said to him, 'Put your sword back into its place; for all who take the sword will perish by the sword. Do you think that I cannot appeal to my Father, and he will at once send me more than twelve legions of angels?' "[27]

This last is important, because almost everyone believed that the Jewish messiah would be a conquering hero who would drive out the occupiers and restore Jewish reign and control over the Temple. Twelve legions of fighting angels would be something like sixty-thousand warriors; that's ridiculous overkill to take one man down from a cross, but twelve legions could easily have swept the Romans (who had far fewer soldiers on the ground) out of Palestine, just as some hoped.

Jesus was saying that he was renouncing violence as an option for himself—and that God was now renouncing it as an option as well.

Thank God. The biblical record is a mixed bag when it comes to God and violence, and many of us these days look at the record of religious bloodshed in the Hebrew Bible with some concern. A God who calls on a father to kill his son, a God who tells his people to slaughter the inhabitants of a land and take it as their own—

this is hard for us to reconcile with the message of peace and broth-erhood we find in much of the Hebrew Bible and throughout the Christian Testament.

We must also wrestle with these texts, though, for Americans have always had a belief in the redemptive power of violence, the idea that while violence may be terrible and war may be hell, often it is the only way to solve a problem. Sometimes it can even lead to good ends—like America itself.

Our country rests upon a foundation of violence against and oppression of others. The land where I sit writing this morning in New Mexico was taken away from the Native Americans who ini-tially lived here by Spaniards, who were overthrown by Mexican nationalists, who were defeated by Texan colonists in battle, before the land they had conquered was annexed by and into these United States. Through the last half of the nineteenth century, the Apache and other Native Americans who weren't willing to accept that history and give up their land peacefully fought in the plains and mountains around me in Indian Wars that were bloody, brutal, and all but genocidal.

I recite this history not to be un-American, but to remind myself—and you—that when we see Alan Ladd portraying a West-ern vigilante who guns down bad guys in *Shane*, or Clint Eastwood as an urban rogue cop who guns down bad guys in *Dirty Harry*, we're seeing the fruits of a philosophy that grows out of our his-tory, a history that suggests that, at least on some level, violence is a solution that works.

So as we talk about violence in film, about sifting films that por-tray their dramatic conflict through fighting and bloodshed for spiritual value, I think we have to use real discernment. We are attracted to violence, we certainly think that it is better for it to be dealt out to others than to us, and particularly today, when warfare tends to take place far away and out of the range of our cameras and reporters (like that missile guided by the CIA operator to its target in the closing scene of *Syriana*), that violence is like a game on a TV screen.

Bloodless. No real targets. No real people involved.

And we forget the lesson of violence we saw in *The Accidental*

Tourist: that violence is done to living people and spreads outward to other living people, hurting everyone in its path.

Three Kings, a movie made about the first Iraq War when it was yet the only Iraq War, features several National Guard reservists who are sorry that they didn't see actual combat. They really wanted to kill someone.

One of the men, Troy (Mark Wahlberg), actually shoots a man—from a great distance—at the beginning of the film. But the others still want to shoot something. When Major Archie Gates (George Clooney) recruits them on a personal mission to steal back some of the gold Saddam stole from Kuwait, they take turns shooting at footballs thrown from the back of their moving vehicle. It's all a game to them.

Then they see the bodies of some of the Iraqi soldiers buried by American bombs, and Major Gates gives a little anatomy lesson to Army Reservist Conrad Vig (played by the filmmaker Spike Jonze): "Specifically, the worst thing about a gunshot wound, provided you survive the bullet, is something called sepsis. . . . Say a bullet tears into your gut. It creates a cavity in the dead tissue. That cavity fills up with bile, and bacteria," and then you are in a world of continuing hurt.

Later when they come to a situation where Gates wants them to project strength but avoid hurting anyone, he has this exchange with Conrad:

> **Gates:** No unnecessary shots, Conrad, 'cause we know what they do.
>
> **Conrad:** Make infected pockets full of bile, sir.
>
> **Gates:** That's right, Conrad, that's what they do.

Three Kings ultimately moves from being a movie about war to a movie about peace; the Muslims that the men encounter in their quest are no different from themselves, although they are supposed to be the enemy. Some of them are frightened, some of them are angry, some of them are evil, and some of them are religious in a way that changes their lives and those around them. By the end of the film, Major Gates and his ragtag band have stopped caring about the gold, and have started caring about seeing the Iraqis who helped them escape make their own escape from Saddam.

It's a degree of complication we don't always see in movies. Many of our most famous war films simplify war to the degree of dramatic conflict between good and evil, and this is understandable—we enjoy seeing the good guys win, and would prefer not to think about those consequences of violence we've mentioned. Yet as early as the beginning of the last century, Mark Twain had considered what happens in war. In Twain's "The War Prayer," a short story that, not surprisingly, went unpublished during his lifetime, a messenger from God translates for a church congregation the prayer they are actually praying when they ask for God's assistance in battle:

> O Lord our God, help us to tear their soldiers to bloody shreds with our shells; help us to cover their smiling fields with the pale forms of their patriot dead; help us to drown the thunder of the guns with the shrieks of their wounded, writhing in pain; help us to lay waste their humble homes with a hurricane of fire; help us to wring the hearts of their unoffending widows with unavailing grief; help us to turn them out roofless with little children to wander unfriended the wastes of their desolated land in rags and hunger and thirst.[28]

Just war theory, which is derived from the writings of Augustine and Aquinas, suggests that war is permissible when it is declared by a legitimate authority, is in the service of a just cause, is pursued with rightful intention after all peaceful means have been exhausted, and ultimately, is undertaken for the cause of peace. There are Christians who support war under these rules of engagement, and certainly even though I call myself a pacifist I'd be hard-pressed not to defend my children against imminent violence. But Robert McAfee Brown says, at the very least, "the burden of proof is always on those who desire to wage war, and never on those who want to avoid war. The initial presumption must always be that war is wrong, and that if there are ever any exceptions to that claim, they can be advanced only when all other options have unequivocally failed."[29]

Other Christian writers such as Dorothy Day, Thomas Merton, and Martin Luther King Jr. were advocates of Christian nonviolence, believing that violence could never be a lasting solution to violence. The Dalai Lama echoes King and others when he writes, "Violence can achieve certain short-term objectives, but it cannot obtain long-lasting ends."[30]

In a world where it is clear that military might does not bring absolute security, violence is no solution, and it may even make things worse.

Christians are encouraged to believe that God alone can bring safety in a broken world, and that peace is a central virtue for Christians, to be pursued even at great personal cost. In pursuing war instead of patiently seeking peace, are we placing our trust in ourselves instead of acceding to God's timing? Are we (as theologian and ethicist Stanley Hauerwas writes) placing our trust in "the lie that we, not God, are the masters of our existence"?[31]

You make the call.

An End to Violence

French film director François Truffaut is supposed to have said that one could not make a true antiwar movie. Like Oliver Stone's *Natural Born Killers*, a satire on violence in American society that some critics found to glorify violence in American society, some argue that any movie that depicts war will necessarily end up glorifying it. Brave men, narrow escapes, you know.

All the same, I think of many great films about war and the impact of war, and I can't imagine how someone could walk away from them thinking that war was a good thing: *All Quiet on the Western Front, Paths of Glory, The Deer Hunter, In Country, Platoon, Full Metal Jacket, Three Kings, Saving Private Ryan*—these are films that may display people acting with heroism, but they also show us the horror, futility, and stupidity of war.

Paths of Glory particularly stands out as an exciting war movie with a noble martial hero that nonetheless demands we think twice about our predilection for war. The film, which came out in the conservative 1950s, was actually banned in France for many years because it depicted the French chain of command in World War I as arrogant, removed from the lives of the common soldiers, and corrupt. In the film, Colonel Dax (Kirk Douglas) is ordered to lead his men against an unassailable enemy position known as the Anthill; in the furious battle, his men are forced to turn back after heavy casualties, and so General Mireau (George Macready) orders that three men must be chosen, court-martialed for cowardice, and publicly executed.

Any three will do.

Colonel Dax knows that the request is unjust; further, he knows that in the heat of the battle, General Mireau ordered his own artillery batteries to fire on his men so that they couldn't retreat. So Dax asks to be appointed to defend the men, and he goes to visit the commanding general, the wily General Broulard (Adolph Menjou). Dax uses every means at his disposal, including attempting blackmail, to save his men, all to no avail. The executions go off as planned, and when it is all over, he hears this from Broulard:

> Colonel Dax, you're a disappointment to me. You've spoiled the keenness of your mind by wallowing in sentimentality. You really did want to save those men, and you were not angling for Mireau's command. You are an idealist —and I pity you as I would the village idiot. We're fighting a war, Dax, a war that we've got to win. Those men didn't fight, so they were shot. You bring charges against General Mireau, so I insist that he answer them. Wherein have I done wrong?

Dax looks at his commanding officer and says, with all the righteousness Kirk Douglas can muster, "Because you don't know the answer to that question, I pity you."

Paths of Glory suggests that men fight and die for no real reason—sometimes just for the satisfaction of the men behind the lines who pull their strings—but it ends with a moment of real reflection and humanity. A bunch of Dax's drunken soldiers hoot as a captured German girl is brought out on stage to sing. Her voice is weak; she is frightened. But some of them recognize the tune, and begin to hum along with her, and again, it is not with a collection of enemies but with a roomful of frightened fellow human beings that the film closes.

If this is not an antiwar movie, it will do until something better comes along.

Some of the greatest films of the late 1960s, even ones filled with violence, stand today as being about the futility of violence. *The Wild Bunch, Butch Cassidy and the Sundance Kid,* and *Bonnie and Clyde* brought to the surface some of the tensions that grew up in American society between the myth of redemptive violence and the dirty reality of the use of violence in Vietnam.

In movies like these, violence isn't sufficient to save the "good" characters (and I use this term advisedly, although what does it mean when three such movies take "villains" as their heroes?). Violence is simply shown to be a mechanism by which greater force ultimately assures the will of those in power. These great films of the era (and others like *The Graduate, The Conversation,* and *All the President's Men*) also question whether American government and American society are always right, love it or leave it. Humility is a necessary condition for thinking about peace. As priest and pacifist Thomas Merton wrote, "It is the refusal of alternatives . . . which makes wars in order to force the unconditional acceptance of one oversimplified interpretation of reality."[32]

Perhaps some wars are unavoidable; perhaps some wars are, even by the definition of Christian theologians, just. But in any case, they should be a last resort, and we should never underestimate the damage and social cost to those on both sides when violence is used.

Ironically, an actor and director who made himself an international star by embodying violence has made one the greatest films about the horrors of violence. In the Italian Spaghetti Westerns like *A Fistful of Dollars* where he played The Man With No Name, in war films, and in the Dirty Harry films, Clint Eastwood's name and image became almost synonymous with the gun as a solution to societal problems. Law and order politicians and regular guys quoted his catchphrases and emulated his steely demeanor.

But in 1992, Clint Eastwood directed and starred in *Unforgiven,* a movie he had waited for years to make, and with this film, he used his life's work as a purveyor of violence to demonstrate why violence is never a good solution, show the human cost of violence, and suggest the possibility that the killer will lose his soul in the process. *Time* magazine critic Richard Corliss noted how *Unforgiven* "questions the rules of a macho genre, summing up and maybe atoning for the flinty violence that made Eastwood famous."[33]

How can a violent movie atone for a lifetime of violent films?

It can make it clear that violence is just a game that men play to try to show they're really men.

And it can show us that there's nothing romantic, or glorious, or even particularly brave about committing it.

Little Bill Daggett (Gene Hackman) is a former gunfighter who runs the town of Big Whiskey (an early allusion to the idea that much of the violence committed in the West was done by drunk men or to drunk men), Wyoming, with an iron fist. When English Bob (Richard Harris) comes to town to collect on a thousand-dollar bounty offered by the town prostitutes against two local cowhands—one of them slashed a whore's face for laughing at his tiny penis—Little Bill beats him within an inch of his life and throws him into jail.

It's an object lesson—like the Children of Israel completely destroying the town of Jericho in the book of Joshua because it was the first town they encountered in Canaan. Little Bill tells Bob that he isn't beating him—actually he's sending a message to any opportunistic gunfighter who might come to Big Whiskey in search of blood money.

Little Bill tried to run his town on the idea that violence would keep out violence. Stanley Hauerwas has written that "we love order, even order that is based on illusion and self-deception. When we say we want peace, we mean we want order."[34] When violence comes into the world, it is a reminder that we live in a fallen world, a chaotic world, a world that can hurt us. Little Bill offered order based on violence, but there is always greater violence, and even the order he offers is flawed. As one character notes, the house Little Bill is building with his own hands, the house he is so proud of, doesn't have a single straight edge, that "he is the worst damn carpenter."

Fortunately, we Christians know a better one.

The conflict is finally joined when William Munny (Eastwood), his old partner Ned Logan (Morgan Freeman) and the so-called Schofield Kid (Jaimz Woolvett) arrive in town to try and collect on the bounty. Will Munny was a bad man once, the worst of the bad, and although his story has been romanticized in the same way English Bob's has (Bob is actually trailed by a writer who chronicles his adventures), he is, when he's full of whiskey, just what the Kid calls him when they first meet: "the meanest goddamn son-of-a-bitch alive." When Little Bill tortures Ned to death for information about their group and has him laid out in a coffin in front of the saloon, Will takes to drinking and comes after him, and he doesn't care who or what gets in his way.

When Little Bill recognizes him, he calls out a challenge: "You'd be Will Munny out of Missouri; killer of women and children."

Drunk as he is, Will still knows who he is and what he's done, and he agrees. "I've killed women and children. I've killed everything that walks or crawls at one time or another. And I'm here to kill you, Little Bill, for what you done to Ned."

Violence in the film isn't depicted as glorious or brave. *Unforgiven* has none of the glossy movie moments we associate with high-concept action films. When Will and his cohorts kill one of the cowboys, a young boy, he lies gutshot, thirsty and screaming, so that Will finally calls out to the other cowboys to take him some water so they don't have to listen to him anymore. By the end of the movie, the Schofield Kid, who has talked about how big and bad he is—or at least wants to be—tells Will he wants no more of the life of violence, and Will understands: "Hell of a thing, killin' a man. Take away all he's got and all he's ever gonna have."

The Kid tries to console himself with the idea that the violence had an underlying purpose, that those they killed had it coming.

But Will Munny knows better. In the saloon, as Little Bill lay waiting for that last shot to come, he had protested, "I don't deserve this. I was building a house," and Will had told him, "Deserve's got nothing to do with it."

Now Will simply says, "We all got it comin', kid."

Violence doesn't have a reason; there's no moral justification for it. It's something people—men, particularly—do because they aren't willing to live in fear. And, as we said, it is the worst offense against justice there is. Thomas Merton wrote that although Christians know that they live in a time of fierce struggle, "this combat is already decided by the victory of Christ over death and over sin. The Christian can renounce the protection of violence and risk being humble, therefore *vulnerable* . . . because he believes that the hidden power of the Gospel is demanding to be manifested in and through his own poor person."[35]

The peace that Christians desire, pray for, and receive from God has nothing to do with the security of our bodies, our homes, or our nation.

But everything to do with our souls.

Chapter Six

The Church and the Christian

What Does It Mean to Be a Believer in Contemporary America?

The Life of Faith and the State of the Church

Sonny (Robert Duvall) is an evangelist, a preacher who tries to serve the Lord as best he can. Like all of us, he's got problems—his fellow evangelist and wife (Farrah Fawcett) is having an affair with the youth minister, and she is simultaneously jockeying to steal their shared ministry out from under him—but he's one hundred percent serious about the work of the spirit, and he has a relationship with God that is, well, personal. "I love you, God," he shouts, "but I am angry with you."

Sonny wants to save, if not the world, at least the souls of those in it. He's not in it for material gain; he doesn't do it for any reason but because he knows in his heart that it's his reason for being. And although he appreciates a pretty face, his hope is not in the things of this world. "I'd rather die today and go to heaven," he says, "than live to be a hundred and go to hell."

But God knows, he's a natural born sinner just like the rest of us, even if he is a "genuine, Holy Ghost, Jesus-filled preachin' machine" saved by the blood of Christ. He gets drunk, takes a swing at that youth minister with a baseball bat, and ends up fleeing to the Louisiana bayou and trying to put his life back together with the grace of God.

The Apostle, which was written and directed by Duvall, is a beautifully made and truly thoughtful movie, but it most assuredly is *not* the story of the men and women of God I know.

144

I don't have any personal knowledge of pastors, priests, ministers, or church musicians who have flipped out and gone after someone with a baseball bat. I can't think of any that have ever had to flee from the law. In fact, although I know a whole lot of priests, pastors, deacons, and assorted other holy folks, and I'm confident that their lives are at least as sin-filled as mine, I'm not personally acquainted with any who have ever been arrested for a violent crime, for molesting a child, or for embezzling from their flock.

I don't for a moment want to minimize the horrible experience of those who have been molested by priests, but from the news coverage, wouldn't you imagine that every Catholic in every parish in America had been a victim? Like the rest of the American media, it seems, the movies have typically shied away from depicting the positive daily routines of Christians and the predominantly redemptive work of the church simply because it generally doesn't make for dramatic stories.

Remember Roger Ebert's comment about angels, in chapter 1? Religious people are most interesting to storytellers (and to the media) when they fail, falter, or fall away from their core values. So we encounter Elmer Gantry (Burt Lancaster) in the film of the same name, an evangelistic charlatan who uses faith to feather his own nest. Or we find the Preacher (Harry Powell, played by Robert Mitchum) in *Night of the Hunter* who likewise makes religion the means to an end, finding the stolen money hidden by his former cell mate. Or we have the repressed and repressive mother (Piper Laurie) in *Carrie* and the small-town preacher in *Footloose* (John Lithgow) who think that Christianity should be sour and joyless, and don't want anyone anywhere ever to have any fun, especially their daughters.

This succession of not-very-Christian Christians may and probably does feel like cultural bias to the Christian members of the film-going audience. Why should American films contain so many hypocrites, opportunists, killjoys, and psychotics identified as religious people? Why, pray tell, aren't there more stories about good Christians who do God's will all day long and say their prayers at night?

Well, I just have one question for you: Have you been talking to my grandmother? Because she is always asking me why instead of writing about sinful people who say bad words I don't write a novel about good Christians living spotless lives.

"*That* would make a good story," she says, smiling her Kewpie smile and crossing her arms.

And I tell her, gently, "Grandma, that would make a beautiful life. But it *wouldn't* make a very good story." I'll spot you *Gandhi* and *Superman*, but most of the time, stories are about flawed people (which is all of us, of course). Otherwise they rarely make very good stories.

At the end of one of her greatest novels, *The Blind Assassin*, Margaret Atwood wrote, "In Paradise there are no stories because there are no journeys. It's loss and regret and misery and yearning that drive the story forward, along its twisted road."[1] And so it is; we yearn for a life of settled contentment, perhaps even a life of faithful service. But we want *stories* where something happens.

So there are lots of movies that contain elements or insights about faith and belief—just not so many that focus on the elements of religion or the settled life of faith. (Or at least there haven't been, although, as we'll see, that is changing.) In this chapter, I'd like to talk about some ways that the church, individual Christians, and faith and belief have been depicted in Hollywood films and what we can learn from them. Then I want to close with a short meditation on the way today's Hollywood seems to be more and more receptive to explicit stories of faith and consider what that might mean for the future.

To begin with, we've got to reckon, of course, with the vast number of films over the years that have suggested that organized religion is a sham, a fraud, or the refuge for scoundrels who want to fit into society. In addition to the baptism scene we noticed in *The Godfather*, where Michael Corleone takes vows to resist sin while having a good half-dozen of his rivals murdered, more recently there's the scene in *Mystic River* where Jimmy Markum (Sean Penn), erstwhile and future criminal, watches his young daughter's first communion. I think all of us would agree that these characters may have a cultural understanding of worship and belief, but that it hasn't permeated their hearts. Should we call them Christian?

Who knows? The murderous father in *Road to Perdition* (Tom Hanks) comes to a Catholic church to confess every time he kills a man, and in that movie he kills quite a few. It would be interesting to know if Michael Corleone ever steps into the confessional. Personally, I doubt it. But perhaps if he did, we might think about him—and the church—differently.

The movies have also shown us those who come to the church because they seek comfort and easy answers, not out of genuine belief. Mickey Sachs (Woody Allen) in *Hannah and Her Sisters* is seeking a reason to live, he needs order and beauty in his life, and so although he was raised as a Jew, he (momentarily) converts to Catholicism. It doesn't go over so well with his parents—when he tells them about his new thing, his mother (Helen Miller) locks herself in the bathroom to cry, and his father (Leo Postrel) asks him, "Why Catholicism? Why not your own people?"

"I thought you'd be happy for me," Mickey tells them. "I never believed in God before and now I'm giving it serious thought."

"You're going to believe in Jesus Christ?" the father asks, exasperated, and Mickey raises his hands, as if to say, I know, I know. Good point.

It clearly isn't going to take—"giving Christianity serious thought" is probably not Mickey's immediate entry to a strong and living faith—but in one brilliant long take, Allen makes his character's attempt to purchase faith eloquent and funny: in a tight close-up, Mickey slowly and methodically unloads a paper shopping bag containing a Bible. A crucifix.

A jar of Miracle Whip.

And a loaf of white bread.

Organized religion is also often depicted as one of the powers that be, as corrupt as any failed government or crooked corporation. In *Primal Fear*, Aaron Stampler (Edward Norton) is in jail for killing an archbishop, but defense attorney Martin Vail (Richard Gere) uncovers a story of priestly abuse and other dirty secrets that might be ripped out of today's headlines.

In some ways, the church has only itself to blame for many of the ways it is perceived. In my faith tradition, a great presiding bishop of the Episcopal Church accused church leaders in the tempestuous 1960s of spending their time and energy rearranging the deck chairs on the *Titanic* instead of dealing with the fact that the world around them was sinking. Similarly, in recent years the slow response of the American Catholic Church in addressing the pain and suffering that some of its priests and other workers have caused parishioners, the revelation that for years bishops simply (and quietly) shuffled around priests who needed to be in treatment (or in jail), and the church's reliance on defending itself through the legal system against past mistakes (which made the church and its accusers antagonists instead of creating a place of holy reconciliation)—created and reinforced the perception of a monolithic church that was interested only in preserving its power and wealth, not in the people who made it powerful and wealthy. The church as corporation, or even as nation-state protecting its borders.

That's the perception we see reflected in movies like *Primal Fear*.

This is of course, as we know, only a tiny part of the story. The Catholic Church has fed the poor, educated children, worked as a great force for good in the world and as a bastion of faith for many. Pope John Paul II was an ardent supporter of reconciliation around the world, and even visited Israel and prayed at the Wailing Wall to throw his vast influence against anti-Semitic versions of Christianity.

But all the same, the headlines definitely make for unified public opinion.

Into this vacuum of negative public perception fell *The Da Vinci Code* and its depiction of the Catholic Church as a power-hungry entity that has kept a big secret from us for, oh, two thousand years. Dan Brown's book sold forty million copies, and Ron Howard's adaptation was not only the most-talked about movie of the year, but the most popular at the box office when it opened. In the movie, two Catholic organizations, Opus Dei and the Vatican, strain to keep secret the story that Jesus and Mary Magdalene were more than just good friends, that Jesus fathered a bloodline with her, and that what we have always called the Holy Grail was this secret, kept secure by the medieval Knights Templar and still kept secret to this very day, circa 2007.

The debunking of the book and movie's claims to factuality have become a cottage industry, and I've had a few words to say about it myself, the most important probably being these, drawn from Saint Alfred (Hitchcock, that is):

It's only a mooo-vie.

A good one, interesting, full of intrigue, mystery, powerful enemies.

But only a movie.

What has caused all the uproar is that people have reacted to the story as though everything it presented was true, and so they have either been outraged or nodded their heads knowingly.

"The world is trying to take away my story of salvation," say some.

"I always knew you couldn't trust the church," say others.

So let's look at some facts. First, the conspiracy about Jesus' kids and grandkids followed to its logical end by Robert Langdon (Tom Hanks), Harvard professor of symbology (and what in the wide wide world of sports is that, anyway?) has been mumbled, written, and lectured about for decades, maybe longer. It's old news. I read *Holy Blood, Holy Grail*, one of the major sources for the book, when I was an undergraduate, which frankly is longer ago that I want to discuss. Jesus stories come and Jesus stories go; I thought about writing a novel about the Priory of Sion in the 1980s, and oh boy, do I wish I had.

But bottom line—the church isn't hiding a secret about Jesus, because it would have come out a long long time ago, and the earliest witnesses we have, stories coming from the first century, don't suggest it. Not that I couldn't love and worship a messiah who married and had children—why in God's name would that matter?—but I don't think he did.

Likewise, while it may be true that official Catholic doctrine devalued the contributions and spirituality of women, what cultures didn't? It's an issue with which all Christian denominations—and many Jewish and Muslim institutions, as well—wrestle. I don't think there was an organized conspiracy, but any impulse to rediscover female voices and early feminine church leaders—and our own recognition that Mary Magdalene was, in the canonical Gospels even, an important disciple of Christ, could be good outcomes to emerge from *The Da Vinci Code*.

Second, the actual villain of the movie is not the Roman Catholic Church, whatever secrets it and Opus Dei may be keeping. The person who tries to kill Langdon and his bestest gal pal Daphne—I mean, Sophie Neveu (Audrey Tautou; sorry, but doesn't it all seem a little like an episode of *Scooby-Doo*?), is Grail-hound Sir Leigh Teabing (Ian McKellen). The albino killer Silas (Paul Bettany) who *thinks* he works for Opus Dei is scary, and he's doing bad things in the name of God, but still, Sir Leigh is the one who directs him to kill Sophie's grandfather. Leigh is the one who brought Opus Dei into all this Grail stuff in the beginning, with the idea all along of implicating Opus Dei in the violence and bringing down the church.

Say it with me: "And I would have gotten away with it, too, if it hadn't been for you meddlesome kids."

Finally, the popularity of the book and the film are evidence that Americans have a real desire to hear stories about Jesus, even this story told in this way, and that gives me great hope. Pastor and writer Brian McLaren has suggested that this hunger for stories like *The Da Vinci Code* may be because those of us in the church haven't done a compelling enough job of telling our story—including our history. When I was growing up, for example, my Southern Baptist pastor used to tell us from the pulpit that the Baptist faith was started by John the Baptist. (If you can, even for a moment, believe that this is true, see me after class.) Too many American Christians believe the Bible and their faith traditions appeared fully formed, or (to quote the words of my friend Martyn Percy, actually quoted in Dan Brown's novel) were faxed from heaven. When someone tells a story that contradicts what they think they know, they're put into a panic. What if they're right? What if I'm wrong? It can't be!

People, people, repeat after me: It's only a mooo-vie.

What *The Da Vinci Code* ultimately says about Jesus is that whatever happened two thousand years ago, people are still willing to live and die for him, and if that's packaged in an outlandish story, well so what? As Roger Ebert wrote:

> Dan Brown's novel is utterly preposterous; Ron Howard's movie is preposterously entertaining. Both contain accusations against the Catholic Church and its order of Opus Dei that would be scandalous if anyone of sound mind could possibly entertain them. I know there are people who believe Brown's fantasies about the Holy Grail, the descendants of Jesus, the Knights Templar, Opus Dei and the true story of Mary Magdalene. This has the advantage of distracting them from the theory that the Pentagon was not hit by an airplane.[2]

Instead of being affronted, it would be good if people realized that *The Da Vinci Code* provides us with a prime opportunity to ask good questions: Where did the collection we call the Bible come from? What is the history of the Christian church? Where did my denomination or faith tradition enter into or fall out of that story? Why do Christians call Jesus the Son of God? Why do I worship him as the Christ?

Not all films treat the church as a corrupt institution populated by hypocrites, fat cats, and politicians, of course. Like *The Apostle*, many movies have featured priests, nuns, or ministers who remain true to their calling to Christ and to the world. *The Mission*, for example, is a film set in colonial times in Latin America, although the issues it addresses remain relevant. In it, Father Gabriel (Jeremy Irons) is priest to a mission built for a community of the Guarani, a tribe who live above the waterfall and beyond the range of Spanish civilization. The church has often been employed by colonizing powers around the world as a civilizing tool, intended to bring people into submission to the secular powers through the imposition of religious power, but Father Gabriel resists that. "If might is right, then love has no place in the world," he says. "It may be so, it may be so. But I don't have the strength to live in a world like that." He refuses to abandon the mission, whatever the cost, and he perseveres in his love for the people he serves until the end.

In *Romero*, Raul Julia portrays the actual Catholic Archbishop of El Salvador, Oscar Romero, a religious conservative who had the audacity to listen to his flock and who thus became a force of justice, speaking against the violence of right and left alike. To the government soldiers killing other El Salvadorans, he says,

I'd like to make an appeal in a special way to the men in the army. Brothers, each one of you is one of us. We are the same People. The farmers and peasants that you kill are your own brothers and sisters. When you hear the words of a man telling you to kill, think instead in the words of God, "Thou shalt not kill!" No soldier is obliged to obey an order contrary to the Law of God. In His name and in the name of our tormented people who have suffered so much, and whose laments cry out to heaven: I implore you! I beg you! I *order* you!

This is, as you can imagine, no way to make friends in high places.

Romero became a fearless advocate for the poor, and with great courage, he brought the church in El Salvador itself into the battle for peace and justice. The real Romero once said that he rejoiced to be part of a church "persecuted for its preferential option for the poor," and said, further, that "a murdered priest is a testimonial of a church incarnate in the problems of the people."[3] As the movie shows, Romero meant what he said; he was himself assassinated in the act of celebrating Mass, but his story remains a powerful lesson that the church can be a force for peace and justice in the world when represented by steadfast servants, and his life and work are still themselves celebrated.

The movie *Dead Man Walking* also tells an inspiring true-life story, about Sister Helen Prejean and her work as chaplain to death row inmates. Sister Helen is berated for her work with convicted killers like Matthew Poncelet, but she sees it as her Christian duty. Surely a savior who preached peace and himself died as a victim of capital punishment would want these inmates to have the opportunity to be redeemed.

"Mr. Percy," she tells the father of one of Matthew's victims, "I'm just trying to follow the example of Jesus, who said that a person is not as bad as his worst deed."

It is a hard, countercultural work she undertakes, and she must struggle both with those outside the prison walls and those within. A prison guard even debates her on capital punishment and whether she should be trying to save men like Matthew Poncelet. He tells her she should be teaching children, not trying to minister to a murderer. "You know what the Bible says: An eye for an eye." But she reminds him of another set of Bible sayings: "You know what else the Bible asks for death as a punishment for? Adultery, prostitution, homosexuality, trespass upon sacred grounds, profaning the Sabbath and contempt to parents."

Sister Helen stays with her task despite these challenges, despite the horror of what Matthew did, and at last, when he is a dead man walking—the call sent out to indicate that a death row inmate is being taken away to his death—she reminds him that he is a child of God and tells him that she will be in the room when they execute him. How hard would it be to be present at such an event? But Sister Helen knows that the rest of the people in the room will be people who hate Matthew, who will celebrate his death, and she wants to be the presence of Christ for him, no matter how challenging that task might end up being.

"I want the last face you see in this world to be the face of love," she tells Matthew, "so you look at me when they do this thing. I'll be the face of love for you."

And so she is. It's not a question of whether Jesus approves of killing; I'm pretty confident he's against it. But Jesus commanded that we love our enemies, go the extra mile, and even from the cross he was loving those who put him there.

All three of these movies feature dedicated clergy who give their lives to—and even for—the church, who prove that they are willing to risk their lives for the people in their charge. In them, we see that the church is not just some holy corporation, and not— please God—some irrelevant social club, but a gathering of people in the name of Christ to do the work of Christ. These three follow an example set by Jesus himself, who said in the Gospel of John,

> I am the good shepherd. The good shepherd lays down his life for the sheep. The hired hand, who is not the shepherd and does not own the sheep, sees the wolf coming and leaves the sheep

and runs away—and the wolf snatches them and scatters them. The hired hand runs away because a hired hand does not care for the sheep.

I am the good shepherd. I know my own and my own know me, just as the Father knows me and I know the Father. And I lay down my life for the sheep. I have other sheep that do not belong to this fold. I must bring them also, and they will listen to my voice. So there will be one flock, one shepherd.[4]

So those are the shepherds, but what is the church? The Nicene Creed speaks of "the holy catholic and apostolic church," but notice how "catholic" isn't capitalized. What catholic means in the creed is *universal*, the sense that all believers of Christ—Roman Catholic, Anglican, Orthodox, and all of the multitude of different Protestant denominations—are the body of Christ, the universal church. "Catholic" includes the Roman Catholic Church, of course, and many of our cinematic examples in this section speak of the Roman Catholic Church, because it is so visible—but the Roman Catholic Church (to its occasional dismay) doesn't encompass the full range of what we mean when we say the word "church."

What is the church? Well, going back to the Gospel record, we can see that Jesus told his followers to remember him; he empowered them to bless and forgive, to heal and to cast out demons. He said that upon Peter (or upon Peter's confession of faith) he would build his church, and Jesus' words indicate that he meant something universal rather than merely local.[5] He gave his followers a commission to go into all the world and preach the good news of the kingdom of God, and the book of Acts and the Pauline Epistles show us a people attempting to do just that.[6] The gathering of those who follow Christ became a group participating in the body of Christ, and with it, they gained the real sense that their fullest knowledge of Christ—and perhaps of themselves—came in community.

While over the years, members of the church argued (early and often), over worship, over spiritual practice, and over virtually everything else (Paul's first letter to the Corinthians reveals a first-century church disagreeing about so many things that he's almost ready to pull his hair out), the universal church of Christ remains. It has been divided, particularly since the Protestant Reformation, and in America, denominationalism and individuality have stolen much of a sense of a holy, catholic, and apostolic church that is universal.

But the body of Christ is more than a set of denominations, and more than a few national headquarters plopped down in Nashville, Louisville, New York. It is where most people encounter God—and find God in the faces and voices of others who also seek God—and it is our link with all others who profess Christ as their way to God. As William Sloane Coffin wrote,

> It seems to me that in joining a church you leave home and home town to join a larger world. The whole world is your neighborhood, and all who dwell therein—black, white, yellow, red, stuffed and starving, smart and stupid, mighty and lowly, criminal and self-respecting, American and Russian—all become your sisters and brothers in the new family formed in Jesus.[7]

Like the little church shown at the end of *Places in the Heart*, filled with black and white, redeemed and sinning, even alive and passed on, the church is the one place in human existence where we are all promised to belong, to God and to each other.

It is an imperfect institution, because it is made up of imperfect people. And still, the church is the place where we meet God, a place where we sow hope for the world.

The Magic of Communion

Our practice throughout this book has been to imagine that we could sift popular Hollywood films for their spiritual meaning, and to assert that even in films that seem to have nothing to do with religion, we could find sprinklings of divinity or life wisdom that have spiritual power. Paul Tillich was one of many theologians who have argued that we can discern "prophetic voices" in works of the culture, and he spoke often about a latent church in which "the ultimate concern that drives the manifest Church is hidden under cultural forms."[8] Although, until recently, faith and belief weren't explicit subjects in most movies, they could still be found, and we have found them.

But there's still one popular form of American film we haven't considered where we can find the concepts of belief and of fellowship (one of the earliest Greek names for the church is *koinōnia* [κοινωνος], which means a fellowship or gathering of the likeminded) powerfully expressed, and that is the Christmas movie. With the exception, maybe, of *It's a Wonderful Life*, which accidentally became "the Christmas movie" because it fell into public domain and broadcasters could and did show it every Christmas season without paying anything for it, it's probably true that (as with most of the other films we've discussed) we can't look to Christmas films for straightforward expositions about belief in God.

And surely, if we take things in Christmas movies at face value, we could end up with an odd understanding of faith. As Brian Bethune notes, we've so badly confused Jesus and Santa Claus that "the inarticulate theolog[ies] of Hollywood Christmas movies make medieval peasant superstition look sophisticated."[9] But all the same, even bad Hollywood Christmas movies show how important our culture finds some of the core components of faith and belief, and we can draw valuable lessons from them.

I blame Charles Dickens. For the current state of Christmas, that is, and I'm not alone. Our friends the Puritans had cracked down on Christmas and some of its more festive elements, and even after they were gone and the prohibitions lifted in England and America, Christmas continued to be a somewhat muted celebration. But Charles Dickens, in a series of nineteenth-century Christmas tales that included "A Christmas Carol," repopularized the celebration of Christmas in a big way, and in "A Christmas Carol" itself, he conflated Scrooge's story of redemption with his willingness to celebrate Christmas. In short, our occasional inability in twenty-first–century America to tell the difference between Christian redemption and Christmas spirit comes to us directly from "A Christmas Carol."

Not that there's anything wrong with that. If the story shows us a grace-driven redemption through supernatural intervention that drives a self-centered lout like Scrooge to treat his neighbors with justice and give to the poor—which it does—then I'm okay with it. As we've seen in these pages, the shape of Scrooge's Christmas makeover is, at heart, the story of religious conversion. Perhaps the reason we're so drawn to Christmas films year after year is that consciously or unconsciously we understand that they are stories about salvation.

The shape of Scrooge's redemption should be very familiar to us through the many adaptations of the story (I'm particularly drawn to the Alistair Sim *A Christmas Carol* and *A Muppet Christmas Carol*, and of course *It's a Wonderful Life* is drawn from "A Christmas Carol" as well), and also through many other Christmas movies, for at the heart of most of them is the central element of Christian faith: the necessity of belief.

We could wish that more Christmas movies perceived the Christmas story to be an essential part of Christmas, and I do. Every Christmas since I was about six years old, I have choked up when Linus steps up into the spotlight and says, "Of course, Charlie Brown. I know the true meaning of Christmas. There were in those days, shepherds in the fields, keeping watch over their flocks by night—"

But still, in a cynical, fast-paced, and overly practical society like ours, the willingness to believe in that which can't be seen or proven empirically takes us a long way in the right direction.

Americans tell pollsters that the vast majority of us believe in God, but what exactly does that mean? We may believe that there is a God (perhaps in the same way I like to say that I believe in aluminum), but do the poll numbers suggest our absolute faith is in God? Are we willing to live and die for that faith?

We all need to have faith in something that gives us worth and to which we can give our lives. It's a human imperative. For some Americans, that faith is given largely to our nation; for some it is largely lodged in science and technology; to some it is in our economic structures; to some it is in consumerism. Richard Niebuhr wrote that typically today when people talk about faith, it is "a mixture of faith in the One God with social faith and polytheism," not what he called "radical monotheism," a radical belief in the One and Living God.[10]

The faith and belief we're going to find in these Christmas movies is not distinctly Christian either, but it does show us countercultural generosity, the power of radical belief, and the way community or fellowship can form around that belief. Through these secular vehicles we can certainly hear the prophetic voices that Tillich talked about.

Miracle on 34th Street contains a number of elements we've already discussed in this book; where there are miracles, we said, there must be God nearby, so who could blame people for confusing the Christmas message with this Christmas story? As in many Christmas stories (from Scrooge's on forward), *Miracle on 34th Street* contrasts the way we live and think in our everyday lives with what is possible at Christmas time, and almost always the everyday comes up wanting.

Kris Kringle (Edmund Gwenn) works as a Santa at Macy's Department Store, and he's very good at what he does. He should be: he says he's the real deal. Not everybody thinks this is possible. As is often true in Christmas films, the vast majority of people can't believe in the possibility of Christmas magic. When Kris Kringle gets locked away as insane and brought up for a hearing, a young attorney, Fred Gailey (John Payne), decides to defend him. "Faith is believing when common sense tells you not to," Fred says. "Don't you see? It's not just Kris that's on trial, it's everything he stands for. It's kindness and joy and love and all the other intangibles."

Belief in Santa, that is, might be a step toward belief in all the other intangibles. And a failure to believe—well that's a slippery slope.

It's important to Fred because he is gaga for Doris Walker (Maureen O'Hara), who has a little girl, Susan (Natalie Wood), and Doris has raised Susan not to believe in frivolous things like Santa Claus. So the element of redemption in the film, the miracle on 34th Street, if you will, is restoring a child's childlike faith. Susan comes around—"I believe . . . I believe. . . . Even though it's silly, I believe"—and ultimately, so does Doris: "I was wrong when I told you that, Susie. You must believe in Mr. Kringle and keep right on doing it. You must have faith in him."

All is well, of course. Belief is restored, Kris Kringle wins his court case, and maybe, just maybe, he was the real Santa after all. To believe in Santa is to believe in the Christmas spirit— giving, celebration, and love—but it is also to have a willingness to accept things you can't see, things that don't make logical sense in the everyday, things that call us to more and better. And that's a faith story that should be familiar to us by now.

Other movies rotate around this question of belief in Santa as well. *The Polar Express*, which apparently will have eternal life as a 3D IMAX extravaganza, centers on a young boy's loss of belief in Santa and his trip to the North Pole on a magical train (which to me would be pretty good proof right there) with a ticket stamped "Believe." The Conductor, who like the Hero Boy is played by Tom Hanks before being digitized, tells the Hero Boy, "Seeing is believing, but sometimes the most real things in the world are the things we can't see."

The Santa Clause (which has also spawned two sequels) stars Tim Allen as Scott Calvin, a busy businessman who—even when he's taken to the North Pole and painfully inserted into Santa's life, has a hard time believing in the concept of Santa; as he flies off in Santa's sleigh, Scott calls out, "Merry Christmas to all, and to all a good night! When I get home, I'm getting a CAT scan!"

Even though he sees, he does not believe, which is not unprecedented. So when Scott arrives at the North Pole, he lets it all hang out. He asks head elf Bernard, "What if I don't buy any of this Santa Clause thing? What if I choose not to believe it?"

Bernard must have heard this question before, because he launches right into an answer: "Then there'll be millions of disappointed children around the world. Y'see children hold the spirit of Christmas within their hearts. You don't wanna be responsible for killing the spirit of Christmas now would you . . . Santa?"

Well, when you put it that way.

Scott's son Charlie (Eric Lloyd), though, believes that Scott is—and can be—Santa. His belief—against the odds, despite the distance between his father's cynical, grasping personality and that of jolly old Saint Nick—makes all the difference. "You helped make me Santa," Scott says to his son, and certainly Scott's ability to tap into his son's need for childlike belief—and his rediscovery of love for his son—allows Santa to keep on flying.

So belief is important, but as we've asked earlier in this book, what do you do with belief? Well, in many of these films, belief leads to action, and belief leads to community. At the end of *Miracle on 34th Street,* a new family unit has been formed—the very definition of comedy, as we noted. Scott Calvin's relationship with his son has been repaired. In *Elf,* belief in the Christmas spirit also repairs a fractured family, and brings together a community united in the Christmas spirit.

Elf, a wildly popular reinvention of *Miracle on 34th Street,* should not be anybody's theological primer, but it does contain some useful elements for people of faith to reflect upon. There's the Elf Code, which you may want to paste inside your Bible or prayer book:

1. Treat every day like Christmas.
2. There's room for everyone on the nice list.
3. The best way to spread Christmas cheer is singing loud for all to hear.

There's the movie's main story, about a human raised by elves named Buddy (Will Farrell), who comes to New York to meet his birth father Walter (James Caan), the usual self-centered I-don't-believe-in-Christmas creep. Scrooge, in short. Buddy gets a job as an elf in Gimbel's department store (and, like Macy's Santa Kris Kringle in *Miracle on 34th Street,* gets in trouble for maintaining that he is the real thing). But he does his best to spread happiness and Christmas cheer wherever he goes—"Treat every day like Christmas"—and at the end of the film, he induces a crowd of cynical New Yorkers to put into practice Elf Code item three: "The best way to spread Christmas cheer is singing loud for all to hear." At last even cranky old Walter sings—"There's room for everyone on the nice list"—and as a result of all this Christmas spirit, Santa's sleigh is able to take flight, and something magical happens to those people gathered together singing. For a moment, at least, that diverse group of people believes in something larger than themselves.

For a moment, that diverse group of people becomes a community. What relationship does "Christmas spirit" have to Christian faith? We might imagine it to be the movement of grace in our lives; our participation in the Christmas spirit makes it possible to see the magic moving, and also to see the gifts the magic brings. Paul Tillich wrote that "in the light of this grace we perceive the power of grace in our relation to others and to ourselves. We experience the grace of being able to look frankly into the eyes of another, the miraculous grace of reunion of life with life."[11] This is what I imagine as I see that group of people uniting in the Christmas spirit—something that catches them up and makes them one.

This communal sharing that grows up out of a group of individuals is a familiar scene in American movies, not just Christmas movies, and it's a necessary corrective for us, perhaps. We Americans pride ourselves on our individualism, we value our privacy, we live behind fences and in gated communities, we sit alone in our steel-walled vehicles while stuck in a herd of other lonely people in their steel-walled vehicles. But as God knew all the way back at the beginning of the world, "It is not good for man to be alone."[12]

Some of my favorite scenes from American motion picture history are those where, all of a sudden, a song breaks out and a group of people come together as one. There are all those great movie musicals: *On the Town, Singin' in the Rain, Shall We Dance?*

But there are also moments when regular people like you and me who can't tap dance find themselves joined by music. The people on the bus in *It Happened One Night*, rich and poor together, singing "The Man on the Flying Trapeze." The great high school dance scene in *It's a Wonderful Life*. And my personal favorite, the feuding rock band Stillwater on their tour bus in *Almost Famous*, suddenly breaking out together into the falsetto chorus to Elton John's "Tiny Dancer."

The image of these diverse people becoming—if only for a moment—one, is for me an image of the sort of community formed in the sacramental life of the church. As the liturgy says, "We being many are one body, for we all share the one bread." Setting aside our differences, setting aside our fears and concerns, we come together to become a community. Then we go back out into the world as changed people, hoping to change the world.

That, ladies and gentlemen, is the church.

Faith and Film: Where Next?

It's not odd that movies about priests, nuns, or archbishops would contain explicit references to faith, to Christian life, and even to God. But even some of the contemporary films we've discussed in this book with secular topics have done the same, part of what many perceive to be a changing attitude in American popular culture toward faith and belief. When in *Million Dollar Baby* it's not the main story line but just an integral part of Frankie's character that he regularly attends mass and argues with the priest about theological issues, it seems to me that we've reached a sea change in the way our culture depicts religion, and it's about time. We depict characters in their love lives and their work lives, in their family lives and their recreational lives.

Why shouldn't we also depict them in their faith lives?

For many years in television, music, comics, and movies any references to faith were likely to be generic ones, intended to be inoffensive and acceptable to the largest numbers of listeners, readers, or viewers. But those days, it seems, are over: in popular music, U-2 and Switchfoot sing recognizably Christian songs about living and believing in the world; in comics, the Fantastic Four's The Thing proclaims himself a Jew by dropping to his knees and praying in Hebrew, the superheroes of the DC universe gather in a cathedral for a service of prayer during the Infinite Crisis, and the X-Men's devoutly Christian Nightcrawler is ordained as a priest; in television, shows about ministers and angels populate network television, while on HBO, Six Feet Under showed the difficulties of a gay man who also believes ardently in Jesus; and at the movies, we see *The Matrix Reloaded* and *The Fellowship of the Ring*, *American Beauty* and *Magnolia*, *Million Dollar Baby* and *Ring of Fire*, and even *The Lion, the Witch, and the Wardrobe*.

Hollywood films from recent years have carried powerful messages of faith for us. *Magnolia* teaches us about the necessity of forgiveness and assures us that God is present in the world; *Constantine* and *Hellboy* tell us that nobody is beyond salvation; *Kill Bill* teaches us that revenge for revenge's sake will destroy us; *Million Dollar Baby* takes seriously the church's teachings on life and damnation; *Syriana* teaches us that we can become servants of evil by failing to question our institutions; *Ring of Fire* tells us that Christianity is not about condemning a person's weakness, but about standing alongside them until through faith they find their strength; *Crash* teaches us that all of us are liable to act out of our worst fears instead of live up to our best selves; *The Da Vinci Code* teaches us that the story of Christ has continuing power to change the world, to throw down institutions that try to hide it or shape it for their own uses.

Although our concern in this book has been to discuss those movies that don't explicitly present the Hebrew Bible, the life of Christ, or the history of the early church, that's not to say that films with explicitly religious subjects aren't worthy of our notice, for certainly they are, although they tend to have more transparency than the films we've been dissecting. Martin Scorsese's *The Last Temptation of Christ* and Mel Gibson's *The Passion of the Christ*, for example, may come from different theological perspectives, but both are sincere and heart-felt attempts to figure out who the Son of God was and is.

The incredible success of Gibson's *Passion*, especially with Catholics and evangelical Christians who rarely attend the movies, has opened the way for similar movies, so we should expect more explicitly religious films in future years, as well as more recognizably religious allegories like the works of C. S. Lewis. But not all movies drawn explicitly from faith stories speak to all people; for my part, I'll take *The Last Temptation of Christ* over *The Passion of the Christ* any day of the week.

One of the problems with transparently religious films is that often they end up appealing primarily to those who already hold the beliefs they contain. If you think that Jesus is the savior of the world and that he was tortured and executed to atone for your sins, then *The Passion of the Christ* will be a powerful and wrenching experience for you. But if you haven't yet reached that point of belief—or if you happen to hold a slightly different one—then it may strike you as a religious snuff film, as some critics have called it.

On the other hand, while Roger Ebert called *The Last Temptation of Christ* "a serious and devout film" that was "likely to inspire more serious thought on the nature of Jesus than any other ever made," if you are offended by the idea that Jesus could have been tempted by the notion of an ordinary life, then all its insights about incarnation won't matter to you.[13] And many people were indeed offended by it, so offended that they picketed theaters where it appeared, so offended that many schools (including the public state university where I taught while I completed my PhD and the private religious university where I taught afterward) refused to allow it to be shown on campus.

If people won't see the story, they can't hear the Story. That's why I've always been drawn to the communication of the truths of faith through dramatic means rather than through more transparent representations or narrowly focused narratives. The dramatic incarnation of spiritual values in a good story makes them accessible to a wider audience, and makes it much more likely that that wider audience will be willing to listen. People who might not choose to see a story about Jesus' crucifixion may plop down eight bucks to see a movie about Spider-Man's.

They may even recognize the correspondences between the two stories and be willing to talk about them.

That's why it gives me hope that audiences and filmmakers seem to be more open than in previous years to stories of faith and religious topics in "nonreligious" films. If we keep our eyes open and our intelligences keen, we will find ever more movies we can study for inspiration and wisdom like the ones we've analyzed here. Of course there will always be naysayers, always be religious institutions and individual believers who condemn movies for being violent, sexual, or sacrilegious, because certainly many of them are.

But as we've seen, they can also be windows to the sacred, and the truth we must realize is that in the modern cathedrals we call multiplexes and in the privacy of our own homes, on our laptops and even on our iPods, more Americans are going to be watching movies than are going to be attending services in our churches, synagogues, or mosques. If they're going to grow spiritually, it's likely that it's going to have to come from something other than a sermon.

Sister Wendy Beckett, nun and art historian, has said that "great art offers more than pleasure; it offers the pain of spiritual growth, drawing us into areas of ourselves that we may not wish to encounter. It will not leave us in our mental or moral laziness."[14]

I think that's true. Good movies do confront us. They force us to think. They won't leave us where we were.

There's a moment in *Magnolia*—a good, confrontational movie—where the gentle nurse, Phil Parma (Philip Seymour Hoffman), tells someone on the telephone that he thinks there's a reason certain movies have certain scenes.

It's because they're *true*, he says.

When we watch movies carefully, hoping to be inspired and to learn wisdom from them, we can recognize those truths in even unaccountable places.

God moves in the world like a projector sending light through film, and suddenly, amazingly, we can see.

Notes

Introduction

1. Quentin Tarantino, *Pulp Fiction* (London: Faber & Faber, 1994), 139.

2. Connie Neal, *The Gospel according to Harry Potter: Spirituality in the Stories of the World's Most Famous Seeker* (Louisville, KY: Westminster John Knox Press, 2002), xi.

3. Office for Film and Broadcasting, "Million Dollar Baby," U.S. Conference of Catholic Bishops, http://www.usccb.org/movies/m/milliondollarbaby.shtml (accessed Dec. 12, 2006).

4. Ralph C. Wood, *The Gospel according to Tolkien: Visions of the Kingdom in Middle-Earth* (Louisville, KY: Westminster John Knox Press, 2003), 4.

5. Urban T. Holmes III, *What Is Anglicanism?* (Harrisburg, PA: Morehouse, 1982), 29.

6. I knew you wouldn't believe me. Read Judges 19:16–20:6.

7. Joseph Campbell and Bill Moyers, *The Power of Myth* (New York: Doubleday, 1988), 16.

8. Scott Brown, "You're Mad as Hell," *Entertainment Weekly* (Aug. 12, 2005): 50.

9. Brian D. McLaren, *The Church on the Other Side: Doing Ministry in the Postmodern Matrix* (Grand Rapids, MI: Zondervan, 2000), 171.

Chapter 1: Faith and Belief

1. H. Richard Niebuhr, *Radical Monotheism and Western Culture* (1960; repr., Louisville, KY: Westminster John Knox Press, 1993), 47.

2. Rowan Williams, *On Christian Theology* (Oxford: Blackwell, 2000), 65.

3. Anselm, "Proslogium," in *Basic Writings*, trans. S. N. Deane (Chicago: Open Court, 1994), 54.

4. Thomas Aquinas, *A Summa of the Summa*, ed. Peter Kreeft (San Francisco: Ignatius Press), 1990, 90.

5. *Anchor Bible Dictionary*, s.v. "Angels" (by Carol Newsom), CD-ROM (New York: Doubleday, 1999).

6. Roger Ebert, review, "City of Angels," *Chicago Sun-Times*, Apr. 10, 1998,

http://rogerebert.suntimes.com/apps/pbcs.dll/article?AID=/19980410/REVIEWS/804100302/1023.

7. "Field of Dreams Scrapbook," *Field of Dreams*, DVD (Universal City, CA: Universal Home Video, 1998).

8. John 1:1; from *The Voice* (Nashville: Thomas Nelson, forthcoming).

9. Willa Cather, *Death Comes for the Archbishop* (1927; repr., New York: Vintage Books, 1990), 50.

10. Gregory of Nyssa, "An Address on Religious Instruction," in *Christology of the Later Fathers*, ed. Edward Rochie Hardy (Philadelphia: Fortress Press, 1954), 269.

11. Ps. 19:1.

12. J. Philip Newell, *Listening for the Heartbeat of God: A Celtic Spirituality* (Mahwah, NJ: Paulist Press, 1997), 24.

13. Augustine, *Confessions*, 7.12.18, trans. Henry Chadwick (Oxford: Oxford University Press, 1991), 125.

14. John Dominic Crossan and Richard G. Watts, *Who Is Jesus? Answers to Your Questions about the Historical Jesus* (Louisville, KY: Westminster John Knox Press, 1996), 76.

15. Aquinas, *A Summa*, 237–38.

16. Josh. 4:14.

17. John 3:2; 4:48.

18. "Making Signs," *Signs*, DVD (Burbank, CA: Touchstone Films, 2003).

19. Howard Clark Kee, "Miracles," in *Oxford Companion to the Bible* (Oxford: Oxford University Press, 1993), 519–20.

20. Dwayne Hastings, "Robertson's Comments on Sharon Shock SBC's Land," BP News, Jan. 6, 2006, http://www.bpnews.net/bpnews.asp?ID=22404.

21. "Making Signs," *Signs*, DVD.

22. Bruce Feiler, *Walking the Bible: A Journey by Land through the Five Books of Moses* (New York: Perennial, 2002), 277.

23. Shyamalan, M. Night, "Making Signs," *Signs*, DVD.

Chapter 2: The Trinity

1. Nicholas of Cusa, *Selected Spiritual Writings*, trans. H. Lawrence Bond (New York: Paulist Press, 1997), 127.

2. Roger E. Olson, and Christopher A. Hall, *The Trinity* (Grand Rapids: Eerdman's, 2002), 15.

3. Anselm, "Proslogium," *Basic Writings*, trans. S. N. Deane (Chicago: Open Court, 1994), 70.

4. Kathryn Tanner, *Jesus, Humanity and the Trinity: A Brief Systematic Theology* (Philadelphia: Augsburg Fortress Press, 2001), 40.

5. A. Cohen, *Everyman's Talmud* (New York: E. P. Dutton, 1949), 19.

6. 2 Esd. 1:30; Matt. 23:37; Luke 13:34.

7. Thomas Aquinas, *A Summa of the Summa*, ed. Peter Kreeft (San Francisco: Ignatius Press, 1990), 170.
8. Athanasius, "Against the Arians," discourse IV, 32.
9. Matt. 17:2.
10. Greg Garrett, *Holy Superheroes! Exploring Faith and Spirituality in Comic Books* (Colorado Springs, CO: Navpress, 2005), 39–43; David Bruce, "Superman," Hollywood Jesus, hollywoodjesus.com/superman.htm.
11. Garrett, *Holy Superheroes!* 51.
12. John 2:14–16.
13. John 19:10–11a.
14. Luke 22: 41–42.
15. John 20:17a.
16. Burton Mack, *Who Wrote the New Testament?* (New York: HarperSanFrancsico, 1996), 304.
17. John 15:13.
18. Mark 14:24.
19. Hendrikus Berkhof, *The Doctrine of the Holy Spirit* (Richmond: John Knox Press, 1964), 9; Rowan Williams, *On Christian Theology* (Oxford: Blackwell, 2000), 107.
20. George S. Hendry, "Holy Spirit," in *The Oxford Companion to the Bible* (New York: Oxford University Press, 1993), 288.
21. Augustine, *Confessions*, 1.1.
22. Mark I. Pinsky, *The Gospel according to Disney: Faith, Trust, and Pixie Dust* (Louisville, KY: Westminster John Knox Press, 2004), 28–29.
23. Rowan Williams, *On Christian Theology* (Oxford: Blackwell, 2000), 126, 120.
24. Berkhof, *Doctrine of the Holy Spirit*, 14.
25. Mark 1:11b.

Chapter 3: Sin and Death

1. Gen. 3:13b.
2. Hildegard of Bingen, *Scivias* (New York: Paulist Press, 1990), 86.
3. Rom. 5:12.
4. Gen. 8:21.
5. Prov. 20:9, Eccl. 7:20.
6. *Anchor Bible Dictionary*, s.v. "Sin, Sinners (NT)" (by E.P. Sanders), CD-ROM (New York: Doubleday, 1999).
7. *Anchor Bible Dictionary*, s.v. "Demons" (by Joanne K. Kuemmerlin-McLean.
8. Elaine Pagels, *The Origin of Satan* (New York: Vintage Books, 1995), passim.
9. John 13:27.
10. Augustine, *Confessions*, 5.18.

11. William Sloan Coffin, "Alex's Death," in *A Chorus of Witnesses: Model Sermons for Today's Preacher*, ed. Thomas G. Long and Cornelius Plantinga, Jr. (Grand Rapids: Eerdmans Publishing, 1994), 263–64.

12. "For I do not do the good I want, but the evil I do not want is what I do" (Rom. 7:19).

13. Rev. 12:9.

14. Walter Wink, *Unmasking the Powers: The Invisible Forces That Determine Human Existence* (Philadelphia: Fortress Press, 1986), 5.

15. J. R. R. Tolkien, *The Two Towers* (Boston: Houghton Mifflin, 1965), 289.

16. Wink, *Unmasking the Powers*, 24.

17. Augustine, *Confessions*, 5. 18.

18. Hendrikus Berkhof, *Christian Faith: An Introduction to the Study of the Faith, 1973*, trans. Sierd Woudstra (Grand Rapids: Eerdman's, 1979), 208–9.

19. Thomas Aquinas, *A Summa of the Summa*, ed. Peter Kreeft (San Francisco: Ignatius Press, 1990, 497; *The 1979 Book of Common Prayer* (New York: Oxford University Press, 1990), 848.

20. Berkhof, *Christian Faith*, 215.

21. The Production Code was a set of guidelines adopted by the motion picture industry regarding what could and what could not be portrayed in films. For three decades, beginning in 1934, all films released were reviewed by the Production Code Administration for violations, which included portrayals of explicit violence or drug use, or suggestions of immorality. See Leonard J. Leff and Jerold L. Simmons. *The Dame in the Kimono: Hollywood, Censorship, and the Production Code* (Lexington: University Press of Kentucky, 2001).

22. Berkhof, *Christian Faith*, 215.

23. Henry David Thoreau, "Civil Disobedience," in *Walden and Other Writings of Henry David Thoreau* (New York: Modern Library, 1950), 637.

24. Hannah Arendt, *Eichmann in Jerusalem: A Report on the Banality of Evil* (1961; repr., New York: Penguin Books, 1994), 35.

25. Romans 3:23 KJV.

26. Unattributed quotations in this section are drawn from material collected in the Ernest Lehman Collection, Ransom Humanities Center, University of Texas at Austin.

27. V. F. Perkins, *Film as Film: Understanding and Judging Movies* (New York: Penguin Books, 1972), 142.

28. Luke 9:24–25.

29. *Book of Common Prayer*, 845.

30. Paul Tillich, *The Essential Tillich*, ed. F. Forrester Church (1987; repr., Chicago: University of Chicago Press, 1999), 166–67.

31. Thomas Keneally, *Schindler's List* (1982; repr., New York: Touchstone, 1993), 159.

32. Roger Ebert, review of "Schindler's List." *Chicago Sun Times*, Jun. 24, 2001, http://rogerebert.suntimes.com/apps/pbcs.dll/article?AID=/20010624/REVIEWS08/106240301/1023.

33. Keneally, *Schindler's List*, 207.

34. Simon Wiesenthal, *The Sunflower: On the Possibilities and Limits of Forgiveness*, rev. ed. (New York: Schocken, 1998).

35. Peter J. Gomes, *The Good Book: Reading the Bible with Mind and Heart* (New York: William Morrow, 1996), 254.

36. Thoreau, "Civil Disobedience," 637.

37. Rowan Williams, *Writing in the Dust: After September 11* (Grand Rapids: Eerdmans, 2002), 33.

38. Ty Burr, "Spielberg's Latest is a Provocative, Probing Thriller." *Boston Globe*, Dec. 23, 2005 (accessed at www.boston.com).

39. Manohla Dargis, "An Action Film about the Need to Talk," *New York Times*, Dec. 23, 2005, movies2.nytimes.com/2005/12/23/movies/23muni .html?ex=1167541200&en=990b1cc52a9abeff&ei=5070.

40. Williams, *Writing in the Dust*, 8.

41. "Where sin increased, grace abounded all the more" Rom. 5:20b NRSV.

42. Coffin, "Alex's Death," 266.

43. John 1:5.

Chapter 4: Grace and Redemption

1. Paul Tillich, *The Essential Tillich*, ed. F. Forrester Church (1987; repr., Chicago: University of Chicago Press, 1999), 195.

2. William James, *The Varieties of Religious Experience* (1902; repr., New Hyde Park, NY: University Books, 1963), 206.

3. Gal. 6:15.

4. 2 Cor. 5:17.

5. Rowan Williams, *On Christian Theology* (Oxford: Blackwell, 2000), 134.

6. James, *Varieties of Religious Experience*, 189.

7. Dietrich Bonhoeffer, "The Cost of Discipleship," in *Dietrich Bonhoeffer*, ed. Robert Coles (Maryknoll, NY: Orbis Books, 1998), 53–54.

8. Jer. 31:33–34.

9. Matt. 6:14–15; Mark 11:25; Luke 18:37.

10. Luke 18:18–23.

11. 1 Cor. 2:14b.

12. Julian of Norwich, *Showings* (New York: Paulist Press, 1978), 179.

13. 1 Chr. 16:34; Ps. 86:15.

14. Matt. 22:37, 39; Mark 12:30–31; Luke 10:27.

15. John 15:12–13.

16. Luke 10.

17. 1 John 4:8.

18. Tillich, *Essential Tillich*, 152.

19. Søren Kierkegaard, *Fear and Trembling*, trans. Alastair Hannay (New York: Penguin Books, 2006), 49.

20. Mark 10:45.

21. James, *Varieties of Religious Experience*, 226–27.
22. Exod. 34:7.
23. Matt. 19:26.
24. Mark 10:21.
25. William Sloane Coffin, *Credo* (Louisville, KY: Westminster John Knox Press, 2004), 16.

Chapter 5: Peace and Justice

1. James 2:14–18.
2. Martin Luther King Jr., "Nobel Prize Acceptance Speech," in *I Have a Dream* (New York: HarperSanFrancisco, 1992), 110.
3. Gustavo Gutièrrez, *A Theology of Liberation: History, Politics, and Salvation* (Maryknoll, NY: Orbis Books, 1973), 11.
4. Matt. 5:17.
5. *Anchor Bible Dictionary*, s.v. "Just, Justice," (by Temba L. J. Mafico), CD-ROM (New York: Doubleday, 1999).
6. Deut. 27:19.
7. Luke 1:52–53.
8. John Dominic Crossan and Richard G.Watts, *Who Is Jesus? Answers to Your Questions about the Historical Jesus* (Louisville, KY: Westminster John Knox Press, 1996), 30.
9. Mark 2:27; Mark 3:4.
10. Luke 4:18–19.
11. Gustavo Gutièrrez. *A Theology of Liberation* (1971; repr., Maryknoll, NY: Orbis Books, 1973), 274–75.
12. Martin Luther King Jr., "Pilgrimage to Nonviolence," in *Strength to Love* (Philadelphia: Fortress Press, 1963), 150.
13. Richard Horsley, *Jesus and the Spiral of Violence: Popular Jewish Resistance in Roman Palestine* (San Francisco: Harper & Row, 1987), 157.
14. Charles Derber, *People before Profit* (New York: St. Martin's Press, 2002), 47.
15. William R. Herzog II, *Jesus, Justice, and the Reign of God: A Ministry of Liberation* (Louisville, KY: Westminster John Knox Press, 2000), 176.
16. Matt. 23:23–25.
17. Roy Herron, *How Can a Christian Be in Politics?* (Wheaton, IL: Tyndale House, 2005), 47.
18. Jim Wallis, *God's Politics: Why the Right Gets It Wrong and Left Doesn't Get It* (New York: HarperSanFrancisco, 2005), 308.
19. Steve Davis, review of "Crash," *Austin Chronicle*, May 6, 2005, http://www.austinchronicle.com/gyrobase/Calendar/Film?Film=oid%3A268912.
20. Martin Luther King Jr., "Letter from a Birmingham Jail," in *I Have a Dream* (New York: HarperSanFrancisco, 1992), 92.
21. David Denby, "Angry People," review of "Crash," *New Yorker*, May 2,

2005, http://www.newyorker.com/critics/cinema/articles/050502crci_cinema?05 0502crci_cinema.

22. Desmond Tutu, "Agents of Transfiguration," in *The Rainbow People of God* (New York: Doubleday, 1994), 118.

23. 1 John 2:9–11 (author's translation).

24. Stanley Hauerwas, *The Peaceable Kingdom: A Primer in Christian Ethics* (Notre Dame, IN: University of Notre Dame Press, 1983), xvii.

25. Num. 6:22, 24:26.

26. *Book of Common Prayer* (New York: Oxford University Press, 1990), 107.

27. Matt. 26:51–53.

28. Mark Twain, "The War Prayer," Wikipedia, http://en.wikisource.org/wiki/The_War_Prayer.

29. Robert McAfee Brown, *Speaking of Christianity: Practical Compassion, Social Justice, and Other Wonders* (Louisville, KY: Westminster John Knox Press, 1997), 106.

30. Dalai Lama, *Ethics for the New Millenium* (New York: Riverhead Books, 1999), 201.

31. Stanley Hauerwas, *The Peaceable Kingdom: A Primer in Christian Ethics* (Notre Dame, IN: University of Notre Dame Press, 1983), 142.

32. Thomas Merton, "Blessed Are the Meek," *Faith and Violence: Christian Teaching and Christian Practice* (Notre Dame, IN: University of Notre Dame Press, 1968), 24.

33. Richard Corliss, "The Last Roundup," *Time,* Aug. 10, 1992, http://time.com/time/magazine/article/0,9171,976223,00.html.

34. Hauerwas, *Peaceable Kingdom,* 144.

35. Merton, "Blessed Are the Meek," 18.

Chapter 6: The Church and the Christian

1. Margaret Atwood, *The Blind Assassin* (New York: Nan A. Talese, 2000), 518.

2. Roger Ebert, review of "The Da Vinci Code," *Chicago Sun Times,* May 18, 2006, http://rogerebert.suntimes.com/apps/pbcs.dll/article?AID=/20060518/REVIEWS/60419009.

3. Jon Sobrino, *Archbishop Romero* (Maryknoll, NY: Orbis Books, 1990), 38.

4. John 10:11–16.

5. Daniel N. Schowalter, "Church," in *The Oxford Companion to the Bible* (New York: Oxford University Press, 1993), 122.

6. Matt. 28:19–20a.

7. William Sloane Coffin, *Credo* (Louisville, KY: Westminster John Knox Press, 2004), 143.

8. Paul Tillich, "Aspects of a Religious Analysis of Culture," in *Essential*

Tillich, ed. F. Forrester Church (1987; repr., Chicago: University of Chicago Press, 1999), 110.

9. Brian Bethune, "The Truth about Christmas," *Macleans,* Dec. 22, 2003, http://macleans.ca/topstories/life/article.jsp?content=20031??? 71986_71986.

10. II. Richard Niebuhr, *Radical Monotheism and Western Culture* (1970; repr. Louisville, KY: Westminster John Knox Press, 1993), 31.

11. Tillich, "You Are Accepted," in *Essential Tillich,* 202.

12. Gen. 2:18a.

13. Roger Ebert, review of "The Last Temptation of Christ," *Chicago Sun Times,* Jan. 7, 1998, http://rogerebert.suntimes.com/app/pbcs.dll/article?AID=/ 19980107/?REVIEWS/801070303/1023.

14. Sister Wendy Beckett, *1000 Masterpieces* (New York: DK Publishing, 1999), i.